Peter Scott: Observations o

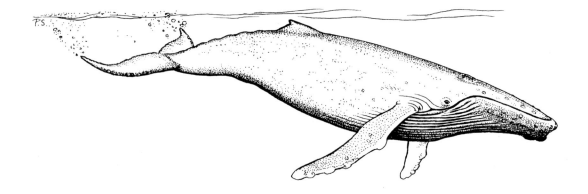

Jacket: *Dawn came over the hill and the first geese left the sand*. 1937. Oil on canvas. Detail at actual size of painting.

The Greylag Geese have been roosting on the high sand of a Westmorland estuary, and as it is the dark of the moon they have not dared to fly in to their grassland feeding grounds during the night. As a result they are hungry, and as soon as it is light enough not to be jumped by a dawn-prowling fox, they fly in over the sea wall to the marshy fields of Brogden where they will spend most of the day.

This picture is an early work. It was painted in 1937. It had the straightforward object of trying to perpetuate a magical moment – but that after all is what most of my pictures have been trying to do.

This page: *Humpback Whale*. 1980. Black ink. About four-fifths of size of drawing.

Title-spread (overleaf): *The coming of winter on the Danube delta*. 1938. Oil on canvas. 36 × 50 in.

In December 1936 I paid my first visit to the Danube Delta. I was looking for Red-breasted Geese, and found a group of 14 of them among a flock of Whitefronts at a place called Gropeni, between Braila and Galati, in Romania.

In 1977 I took my wife Philippa to the precise place – and our Volkswagen had a puncture there. It had greatly changed, and the grass fields were all ploughed. There were no wild geese.

But my first visit, described in some detail in my book **Wild Chorus**, was too late in the season. The snow already covered all the grass and the geese were leaving for Bulgaria and perhaps Greece. The flood water was still unfrozen, and a single skein of Whitefronts was all that I saw on that last morning. But it was a memorable dawn.

PETER SCOTT

OBSERVATIONS OF WILDLIFE

PHAIDON · OXFORD

Phaidon Press Limited, Littlegate House, St Ebbe's Street, Oxford OX1 1SQ

First published 1980
Paperback edition 1986
© Phaidon Press Limited 1980

British Library Cataloguing in Publication Data

Scott, *Sir* Peter, *b. 1909*
    Observations of wildlife.
    1. Animals in art
    2. Water-color painting – Technique
    I. Title
    751.4'22   ND2280

ISBN 0-7148-2041-5 (hbk)
        0-7148-2437-2 (pbk)

Printed in Portugal by Printer Portuguesa, Lisbon

The works reproduced in this book are all in private collections. For reasons of security, locations and names of owners have not been given. The publishers would like to thank the following organizations and individuals who have kindly made available colour and black and white photographs for reproduction:

Arthur Ackermann and Son Ltd; Mr E. Butler-Henderson; Mrs James Fisher; Mr Michael Garside; the Oxford University Press and Mr Stanley Cramp, chief editor of Birds of the Western Palearctic Ltd; the Royal Society for the Protection of Birds; Mr Julian Royle and Royle Publications Ltd; Shell U.K. Oil; Mr Max Williams; the World Wildlife Fund.

The publishers would also like to thank Messrs Ackermann, Messrs Sotheby and *Country Life* for helping them to make contact with owners of pictures. Many owners wrote or telephoned, offering their pictures for reproduction, and their kindness and help are gratefully acknowledged. The publishers regret that for reasons of time and space it was not possible to include all these pictures in the book.

Contents

Acknowledgements

This book is dedicated to all those
who have encouraged and inspired
me since childhood, but principally to:

PHILIPPA

who for the last thirty years has helped most.

In a book of pictures painted over nearly half a century, how is it possible to acknowledge my gratitude to all those people who have helped me? The number is too great, and to pick out individual names would be inevitably invidious. In saying 'thank you' more collectively I should like to begin by thanking all the people who have collaborated with me in the making and presenting of my various creative works whether it be drawing and painting, putting television programmes on the air, laying out Wildfowl Centres, or simply trying to make conservation organizations work. Then I'd like to thank all the people who keep those creations going. And finally I want to thank all those who have written to me in appreciation of my work. I believe I have answered most of their letters at the time, but some, I fear, may have gone unanswered, and I would hate anyone to think I am ungrateful for those friendly messages of good will. An appreciative letter from a stranger is one of the most heart-warming things I know.

It is perhaps possible to be more specific in my thanks when it comes to the creation of this book, and in particular I should like to pay tribute to Michael Garside. It is no exaggeration to say that but for him it might never have been completed at all, let alone met the final deadline of the long-suffering publishers. Mike has been my secretary, personal assistant, glider-crew, and friend for twenty-five years. His contribution to the organization of my life from day to day has been indispensable to my creative output – including *Observations of Wildlife*.

P. S., Slimbridge, February 1980.

Foreword
by H.R.H. The Duke of Edinburgh K.G., K.T.

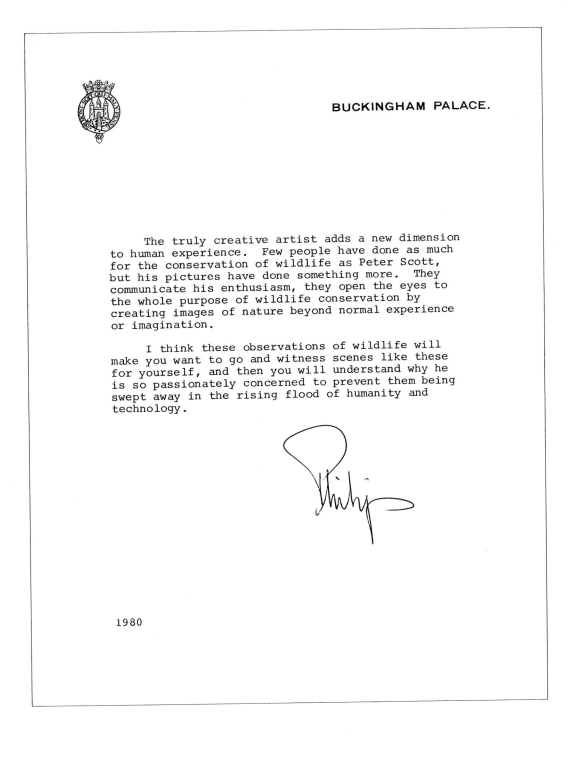

BUCKINGHAM PALACE.

The truly creative artist adds a new dimension to human experience. Few people have done as much for the conservation of wildlife as Peter Scott, but his pictures have done something more. They communicate his enthusiasm, they open the eyes to the whole purpose of wildlife conservation by creating images of nature beyond normal experience or imagination.

I think these observations of wildlife will make you want to go and witness scenes like these for yourself, and then you will understand why he is so passionately concerned to prevent them being swept away in the rising flood of humanity and technology.

1980

Preface

Better remain silent and be thought a fool than open mouth and remove all possible doubt.

CHINESE PROVERB

This is a book of pictures, but it is, so my publishers tell me, the kind of book that has to have words as well as pictures. When I have said what I want to say in paint that should be the end of it, but now I have to say some more in written words. J. K. Galbraith said, 'anyone who says he finds writing easy is either a terrible writer or a terrible liar.' I do not find writing easy, nor is application one of my outstanding qualities. Like a twittering bird, my mind too often flits from twig to twig – from one fascinating subject to another.

I suppose the main reason for putting together words for this book is to convey some sort of impression of the person who painted the pictures – something of the philosophy of this particular painter-naturalist. However, I am not an introspective man and I am doubtful how well I know myself. 'It is as hard', said Thoreau, 'to see one's self as to look backwards without turning round.'

Back in 1961 I wrote an autobiographical book in which I said that I was the happiest man I knew – and the luckiest. Now, 19 years later, I have no reason at all to revise that assessment. It still applies. After 28 years of marriage I am still in love, I am still loved, I am still able to listen to music, and still able to do the things I like doing best – watching and painting and drawing wild nature, on land and in the sea. I still think that I do not deserve such good luck, but not to recognize it, and rejoice in it, would be unforgivably churlish.

The part that my wife, Philippa, plays in my life is central. She is my principal adviser. She manages my business and financial affairs. She cooks my food and looks after me and the house. Although both of us have Scottish ancestry, she seems to have inherited more of the proverbial thrift of the Scots than I have, which at least to some extent counteracts my own tendencies to gross extravagance. Without her I'd be lost – and bankrupt. We have three grown-up children and three grandchildren, all of whom still visit us regularly. We are also blessed with many friends. It was William Shenstone, I believe, who once said: 'Increasing years cause us to esteem fewer people and to bear with more.' I understand what he meant.

Wind in the reeds. 1960. Oil on millboard. 10 × 8 in.

When my autobiographical book was about to be published I was required to produce a picture for the dust jacket. For the purpose I painted three small pictures of which this was one. It was not selected, for a number of reasons, though in some ways I liked it better than the one that was.

When we wish people health and happiness it seems to suggest that the two are in some way linked – that health is a prerequisite of happiness – but I know that this is not so, because the human spirit can rise magnificently above ill-health, as I have many times seen. I have been exceptionally fortunate in my health, and, with advancing years, I have begun to take rather more care of it than I used to do. Each day that I am at home I swim twenty lengths of the little indoor swimming pool which Philippa built for me, out of a windfall legacy, with the express object of prolonging my life (and to which our eldest daughter, Nicola, brought our grandchildren to learn to swim).

So, I am on the whole healthy and happy and lucky, and an optimist. It has been said that, to be an optimist these days, you have to

The Blue Goose. 1953. Oil on canvas. 25 × 30 in.

Ornithologically speaking the picture, painted in 1953, may seem enigmatic. The blue phase of the Lesser Snow Goose is often referred to as the Blue Goose; but that is not the bird in this picture. The basic outlines of the birds are those of Pink-footed Geese; and occasionally in the flocks of that species there are whitish or very pale grey birds which are leucistic mutants; that is to say, they have less pigmentation, though they are not 'albinos'. It might be possible that such a bird, in the evening light, could look blue. But in fact it is a case of nothing more than artistic licence. I liked the basic burnt sienna colour of the three birds and decided that the fourth would look very nice in blue. I do not think that Picasso's blue period had much to do with it. My wife liked the picture so much that I gave it to her, and it has hung over our fire place in the studio at Slimbridge ever since.

be illiterate. To a considerable degree I am illiterate, in that I read very little. As a child I was a late reader and a late developer. Nowadays people say I suffered from dyslexia, though at that time the condition had not even been given a name. Some considered I was backward because of being left-handed, which I have been all my life. I still read very slowly, and I cannot read and paint at the same time – two good reasons, I claim, for being illiterate. But whenever I start reading a book, I find myself getting quite carried away by it and usually enjoy it enormously.

'Life, liberty and the happiness of pursuit' was proposed in a toast not long ago by Sir Hugh Casson. Certainly pursuits of various kinds may be the best key to happiness. But life is not only about happiness. It is about achievement and fulfilment – and harmony and peace. I believe that it is about man's proper relationship with nature – with our planet and with the other living things that share it with us. I am concerned with the personal relations between individual people and individual animals, from household pets to wild creatures. We keep two dogs in our home; we love them very much and they are excellent watchdogs; but most important of all they provide a kind of evolutionary perspective which puts us, as humans, in our proper place in relation to the rest of the animal kingdom. This relationship, which man has so frequently and flagrantly abused, is one of the most important elements that needs cultivating in our evolutionary progress towards a higher state of civilization.

With advancing years I find that my memory has become rather patchy, and there are times when past detail is more easily invented than drawn from a reluctant memory. Our dear and greatly lamented friend, Nancy Legendre, with whom we used to stay in Washington D.C., was a delightful fellow traveller on the cruise ship *Lindblad Explorer*. We taught her to snorkel on coral reefs and she introduced us to the very useful word 'confabulation'. It means something which you think you remember happening, though you're not quite sure; but after you have recounted it a number of times you are absolutely positive that it happened – of course it did. Many of the reminiscences in this book may well be confabulations, and many of those who read them will know, as they read, that that is what they are. In the words of the old saying, 'to be clever is to believe only half of what you hear. To be wise is to know which half.'

Chapter 1   Painter-Naturalist

'Painting is a science and should be pursued as an enquiry into the laws of nature.'

JOHN CONSTABLE

My father wrote a letter to my mother from the tent in which he and his companions died on the way back from the South Pole. In it he said, 'make the boy interested in Natural History: it is better than games. They teach it at some schools.' My mother encouraged me to be interested in Natural History, and as she was a sculptor, she encouraged me to draw. I cannot remember a time when I was not interested in animals; nor can I remember a time when I did not draw, beginning in the days when I lay face-downward on the nursery floor. By the time I was five years old, I was already a committed naturalist and a committed artist who spent long hours drawing.

In those days it was with pencil and coloured crayons. My godfather, J. M. Barrie, had made me a Life Fellow of the Zoological Society of London as a christening present, and so the subjects were zoo animals, flowers and birds, first-world-war aeroplanes, zeppelins, dinosaurs, lizards, caterpillars, and more birds. The drawings were not very good, either as records of the appearance of the subject or as primitive art. But then I was planning to be a biologist, and it was useful to be able to draw specimens. My first published drawing was of a fully-fed Privet Hawk Moth caterpillar in a book on insects. At school I made drawings for a bird book written by a contemporary with whom I shared many ornithological adventures. It was published by another contemporary's father, and because it was the third schoolboy's idea, the book was 'by Three Schoolboys'.

While at university I became a wildfowler and drew and painted my quarry, as the cave-men drew and painted on the walls of their homes. But towards the end of my university years I had begun to wonder whether, in a scientific career, I might be going to miss out on the humanities, and perhaps after all I should be a professional painter. If that was a right course, then perhaps I should not only study 'History of Art & Architecture', which I had done in a last year at Cambridge, but I should also learn my trade by going to art school, which I did first in the State Academy in Munich and then at the Royal Academy Schools in London.

Pinkfeet gliding out to the loch. 1975. Oil on board. 24 × 20 in.

The geese are coming out from the field where they have been feeding, to drink and wash in the loch, before returning for more gleaning on the autumn stubbles. As they lose height, they make, I hope, a satisfying pattern.

Honkers coming in to winter floods. 1979. Oil on canvas. 20 × 30 in.

These Canada Geese are coming to roost in a place where they regularly spend the night. They are confident, and as they sweep round to head the light southerly breeze one or two of them begin to 'whiffle' in order to lose height quickly. It is a kind of 'falling leaf' manoeuvre. These remarkable aerobatics often involve the bird for a second or more in inverted flight, when the outstretched legs point directly upwards. I have watched many hundreds of wild geese 'whiffling', but have never seen one complete a roll. They always seem to reverse the direction of rotation so that it is a half roll one way followed by a half roll back again. Once in one of Heinz Sielmann's films, I found he had recorded a complete roll performed by a White Stork.

Canada Geese – often called 'Honkers' in North America – were first introduced into England by King Charles II in 1678. In 1978 there were some 20,000 of them in Britain. The landscape could be on either side of the Atlantic but it was commissioned from the United States.

By then Wild Geese had captured my imagination, and if the two words are printed with initial capital letters, this is merely to indicate that they had become, and have remained, a kind of obsession. Wild Geese and, as I was afterwards to learn, their close relatives, Wild Swans, are very special birds because their society is based on a permanent pair bond and a family life which keeps the young with their parents until breeding time comes round again. It took me a little time after I had learned these things before I decided to give up all shooting. I have not fired a gun for 32 years.

Meanwhile there were many other special things about Wild Geese. As birds go, they are rather intelligent. They make long and still incompletely understood migrations, they fly in skeins at dawn and dusk, calling most tunefully, and often they gather in vast aggregations which constitute, in many countries, the finest wildlife spectacle still to be seen. All of these things give the Wild Geese and Wild Swans a special magic in the hearts and minds of most people who have come to know them well over a long period of time. It is more than 50 years since I first fell under their spell, and I remain totally addicted to their

Pinkfeet flighting in morning mist. 1971. Oil on canvas. 20 × 24 in.

The sun is well up but the fog has not yet burned off. However, the geese have begun to flight in. When the great birds are coming towards you there is always excitement, whether you are there to enjoy their proximity or to try to kill them. Any bird that is flying towards you is more exciting than one that is flying away. And of geese this is particularly true. If it is coming closer you will see it better, you will photograph it better, and if you have unfriendly motives it will be in greater danger.

Mist over the mudflats – Canada Geese. 1971.
Oil on canvas. 28 × 36 in.

**Having completed and signed and dated
this picture, I believe I have said almost
all there is to say about it. My fascination
for back lighting, for wet mud, for mist,
and for birds flying through it, is here
displayed. Whether the final statement is
meaningful is for the viewer to judge.**

magic. So, when I went to learn to paint, it was largely to be able to
paint my Wild Geese better.

My earliest paintings were in watercolour, which is, I find, a very
difficult technique. So difficult indeed that when I am using water as a
medium, I am constantly adding opaque whites to correct my mistakes. 'Body-colour' can make for greater exactitude but it tends to
produce a 'muddiness' which is much less attractive than the pure
transparency of the watercolour paints. Once 'body-colour' is involved, you are technically working in 'gouache', and if you want even
more body to the paint you must move into 'acrylic' (if you want to
remain water-based) or into oils. In oil painting the technique is much
simpler than in watercolour, in that covering over what has been
painted before is perfectly normal and indeed part of the process. I am
primarily a painter in oils.

Pinkfeet against an autumn sky. 1969. Oil on canvas. 18 × 15 in.

The picture is a straight exercise in conveying atmosphere and forward movement – atmosphere by the tones of the near and the far birds, and motion by the patterns of their formations.

Clearly they are flying from left to right – but the question is, 'are they going fast enough?'

People often ask me 'what is your favourite bird', and I always have to answer with a Wild Goose or Swan. But which? Pinkfoot, Barnacle, Lesser Whitefront, Redbreast, Ross's, Nene, Bewick's . . . ? Which indeed? For long years I replied 'Pinkfoot' without hesitation, but more recently 'Bewick's Swan' seems at least to have drawn level as an answer.

In between, each of the others has staked its claim in my heart.

Pink-footed Geese coming in to stubble. Date unknown. Black ink. Actual size of drawing.

Someone told me that oil paints were not a suitable medium for depicting birds – and I felt like showing that it was not so. Of course I had seen reproductions of oil paintings by the great Swedish painter Bruno Liljefors, which showed that it could be done, and I was greatly impressed by his work. But there were other things to draw – portraits of people as well as portraits of birds. And drawing portraits of people demands that the end product should be a likeness. I soon realized that most bird painters had failed to produce the standard of likeness which would make the viewer of a human portrait able to recognize who had been the model. Painting a portrait so that you could only recognize some unidentifiable human being is simply not good enough for an aspiring portrait painter. In the case of birds I found that many paintings left the viewer in doubt as to what *species* of bird had been depicted, let alone which individual. So there seemed to be an endless task in upgrading the standards of truth in bird painting. And after birds, coral reef fishes and whales under water. My pictures have been exhibited in one-man shows down the years at Ackermann's Galleries in Bond Street – for the first time in 1933 and most recently, 42 years later, in 1975.

I think it was after my third exhibition at Ackermann's that the Galleries proposed to make a print of one of my oil paintings. It was a great success and there followed a series, at first almost annually, but later at longer intervals. So far 31 pictures have been reproduced in limited editions, numbered and signed. When the first one came out I was warned that this was rather an unorthodox thing for a serious painter to do, and it would almost certainly damage my reputation. Maybe it did that, in some quarters, but I found that it did the opposite in others, and I became better known as a painter of birds as a result.

Whooper Swans at morning flight. 1967.
Oil on board. 20 × 26 in.

As in most of my pictures, the place
is imaginary, but somewhere in the
British Isles, probably in Scotland.
Soon after dawn the swans will
leave their roosting place on the
loch and head up river to their
feeding fields. In this case they are
following the west bank, and four
Mallard are flying with them.

There is a special challenge in
painting swans against the light.
Some of it shines through the
feathers, some is reflected up from
the water, some down from the sky.

Little more to tell about those 23
Whoopers, except that they may be
part of the 5,000 Icelandic-bred
population, of which 4,500 are believed to spend the winter in Britain
and Ireland. As yet we do not know
what proportion of our winter
Whoopers come down from Scandinavia and the USSR. At present
there is only a handful of records of
Whoopers breeding in Britain, and
it seems probable that some of
these may be wounded birds whose
mates have stayed behind to keep
them company.

Canada Geese coming in to land. 1946. Drypoint. 9 × 14 in.

These are two in a series of drypoints that I made, drawing with a steel stylus directly onto a copper plate, in 1946 when I was in New York for an exhibition of my paintings at Arthur Harlow's Galleries on 57th Street.

In my youth at school I used to make etchings and dry-points. Being an impatient boy, I preferred the dry-points, which only require you to scratch a copper plate with a sharp steel needle. The etchings are more laborious to produce. The copper plate is coated with wax and the needle merely removes the wax so that the copper can be eaten away by acid. This all took much longer before I could see a result. The advantage, of course, of these techniques was that I had a number of copies which could be sold in a limited edition. More recently I have tried another technique to produce several rather similar but nevertheless individually different works of art. This is the 'xerograph', in which twenty copies of a black and white drawing, originally made on white paper, are reproduced in a copying machine on different tinted papers. Each of these I then colour by hand so as to produce a gouache drawing based on the same design but with quite different colorations. I usually limit these editions to twenty.

My work has included pictures and line drawings to illustrate books, identification books in particular, letterheads, and designs for symbols, logos, medals, coins, and ties. One very successful identification book which I drew first in black and white and later in a

Mallard dropping in. 1946. Drypoint. 10 × 8 in.

coloured version is the *Key to the Wildfowl of the World*. This was produced in 1948 and is still in print today. Fortunately the patterns of the different species of wildfowl do not become out-of-date. Evolution does not change them so rapidly. The same applies to fish, and the *Fishwatcher's Guide to the Coral Reefs of the Western Atlantic*, printed on waterproof plastic so that you can take it under water, has sold well for many years.

Both these books are field guides in that they can be carried in the pocket. The inventor of the field guide principle was the Swedish/American painter, Roger Tory Peterson. His first field guide was to the birds of eastern North America. I am not sure whether he realized the extraordinary revolution that he was about to create by publishing this book. Subsequently field guides of the same type, under the aegis of the same publishers and of Roger himself, have been issued on all manner of subjects from birds to amphibia, and from footprints to the night sky. In my view this invention was a major step in human progress. It provided an entirely new series of outdoor objectives, which are basically environmentally friendly, and in tune with conservation.

This drawing of two Bewick's Swans is the Wildfowl Trust's logo.

Opposite: *The Northern Swans*. 1952. Oil on canvas. 30 × 25 in.

This picture was painted in 1952 as one of the illustrations for the first volume of *The Waterfowl of the World* by Jean Delacour (Country Life, 1954). I now know more about the shapes of swans than I did in 1952, and I find that I made the necks too long in all of them, and the bills rather too heavy. However, in relative length one to another for comparative purposes they are still useful, and perhaps fulfil the purpose of the plate.

Top row, left to right: immature and adult Whistling Swan, immature and adult Bewick's Swan, adult Jankowski's Swan.

Bottom row, left to right: adult and immature Trumpeter Swan, immature and adult Whooper Swan.

Left: *Pintails piling in*. 1957. Oil on board. About 24 × 18 in.

This small picture was used as a cover for my *Coloured Key to the Wildfowl of the World*. The marsh and its reeds could be almost anywhere in the northern temperate regions of the globe, and so could the Pintails, for the species is circumpolar, and probably ranks as the second most numerous of the duck species after the Mallard. For bird-watchers in Britain, however, it is more interesting than in America or the Middle East, as it is a rather rare breeding bird and only in a very few places are large concentrations to be seen in winter. At times, however, thousands may be seen together at three of the Wildfowl Trust's centres – Welney, Martin Mere and Caerlaverock. There are some hundreds at Slimbridge in most winters.

Being able to put a name to an animal or a plant has a special appeal, and if the differences are small and require careful observation to determine them, the activity is all the more appealing, taking on a kind of 'crossword puzzle' fascination which can easily become compulsive. With luck it can, and often does, lead to a life-long enthusiasm for the subject, making Roger Peterson's invention a major contribution to the relationship between man and the rest of nature.

I am sometimes asked about my motives in painting. Why do I do it? What am I trying to do? What are my objectives? Well, I do it because I like doing it. I do it because I can't help doing it. I like to draw or paint something every day of my life, though I don't always manage to do it. And the first of my objectives is to give pleasure to people – as many people as possible, some possibly not yet born. I like to draw things that have excited me, to reflect my own enthusiasm for nature in general and especially for birds (and fishes and whales). I like to record, whenever possible, aspects of their behaviour and their

Two Red-breasted Geese. Date unknown. Black ink. About seven-eighths of size of drawing.

Opposite: *Red-breasted Geese over a Romanian wheatfield.* 1974. Oil on canvas. 28 × 36 in.

The rolling country just to the south of the Danube delta is the main winter feeding ground of most of the Red-breasted Geese in the world. They crop the winter wheat shoots (without damaging the subsequent crop) in vast hedgeless fields of several hundred acres each. We once found a single field of over 1,000 acres. After a light snowfall and a little sunshine, the furrows in the fields are picked out in undulating dotted lines, which indicate the contours that sometimes make it possible to stalk the geese for photography. Good photography of Redbreasts has been one of the main objectives of our various expeditions, as winter flocks of them have very rarely been closely approached and it is extremely difficult to persuade them to land near a photographic hide. The flock in this picture may land back with the few down in the hollow that did not take off. Among the 102 Redbreasts there are, on this occasion, 10 Whitefronts.

Below: *Redbreasts coming from Lake Sinoie to join the Whitefronts.* 1975. Oil on board. 15 × 18 in.

There are probably fewer than 20,000 Red-breasted Geese in existence – possibly not much more than half that number. But many thousands may be seen together in winter around the Romanian lakes which lie to the south of the Danube delta channels. They consort during the winter with a much larger assemblage of White-fronted Geese. The Whitefronts tend to flight first into the fields by the lake, and when they have landed the Redbreasts follow, thereby using the greater watchfulness of the grey geese to their own advantage. In this picture six Whitefronts have been the pathfinders when the geese return after their mid-morning drink on the lake.

Lake Sinoie was formerly salt water, being separated from the Black Sea only by sand bars. But recently it and its neighbouring lakes have been sealed off to provide fresh water for irrigating the vast wheatfields. This in turn means that they freeze over much sooner in winter, and the foxes can walk out onto the ice, giving the geese a much less secure roosting place.

biology as well as their appearance. I like to help to educate others to enjoy them, thereby enriching their lives too, and at the same time advancing the cause of conservation. And finally, I have to earn money in my profession, and to have been able to do so for almost half a century has been another piece of good fortune.

Another question is how I set about making an oil painting. There are two different ways in which my process of thought is started. In the first I decide to paint a picture. At the back of my mind is some vague concept of a subject, but I have no idea how I am going to lay it out. I select a plain white canvas and set it on the easel, stand in front of it, squeeze out some paint (usually blue or brown) onto a paper palette and simply let my left hand go to work. The picture takes charge and goes its own way. That is, I suppose, the purest way of painting, and occasionally those pictures come out quite well. They have, after all, a certain spontaneity.

Opposite: *Fulmars at sea.* 1950. Oil on canvas. 30 × 20 in.

This picture was painted as a commission for the frontispiece of James Fisher's admirable monograph on the species. In former times Fulmars had a limited breeding range in Britain, confined to steep cliffs on islands off the northern parts of Scotland. However, the practice of gutting fish at sea produced a substantial food supply from fishing vessels of all kinds, which was exploited by the Fulmars, and that led to a great increase in their numbers, and an extension of their breeding range. In my picture I have tried to give some indication of this interesting feature of Fulmar biology.

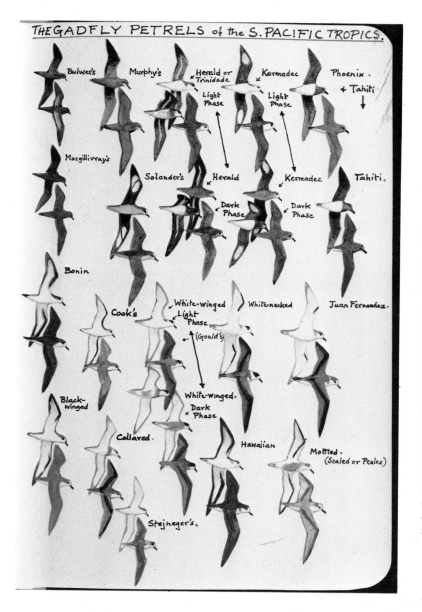

Gadfly petrels of the tropical South Pacific. 1973. Watercolour in diary. Page 8 × 6 in.

In 1973 Philippa and I made a marvellous voyage in the *Lindblad Explorer* across the South Pacific, from Puerto Mont in Chile to Fiji, calling at Juan Fernandez, Easter Island, Pitcairn Island, the Tuamotus, the Marquesas, Tahiti, Bora Bora, Raiatea, Rarotonga, and Tonga. The journey took five weeks, and we had a good many days at sea. During these we spent much time bird-watching and flying-fish watching. Often there were gadfly petrels in sight. These are larger than storm petrels and smaller than most shearwaters. But they are very difficult birds to identify, because many of them breed only on one or two islands in widely different parts of the ocean, so that at any time one may see one of some twenty different species. Using all available books, I put together a page of drawings in my diary which were strictly comparable so as to help me and the many other ornithologists on board to identify these difficult birds when we saw them sweeping past low over the water, often at a considerable distance from the ship. In the event we saw the seven species marked with a red spot after the name.

A sketchbook page. 1949. Pencil and blue pen. 11 × 14 in.

The top half of the page is a view of the River Kennet in the Perry River region of Canada's Northwest Territories. Underneath are some drawings of Blue and Snow Geese.

But more often I set out to paint a commission, which means that the picture must have some preordained elements – some features which the commissioner required in the picture. This may involve a series of rough pencil drawings, usually smaller than a post card, to get a basic composition into my head before I start. It may call for aids of various kinds, field sketches and photographs to remind me of the place and the creatures I am going to paint, although most of my painting is done from memory. At this early stage there are major decisions to be taken before the painting itself can begin. For example, what kind of canvas should it be painted on? A rough one or a smooth one? Should it be painted simply with brushes straight onto the primed canvas, or should I consider using palette knives? Should I put on a background of sky, or a layer of underpainting? Or should I prepare a rough stippled background on which to paint? (This last, by

Summertime in the Canadian Arctic – Ross's Geese. 1949. Oil on canvas. 20 × 30 in.

With Paul Queneau and Harold Hanson, I went to the Perry River in the summer of 1949 to study the little-known Ross's Goose on its breeding grounds. We camped at the foot of a small hill overlooking a small lake not far from the river, where after a few days the local Kogmuit Eskimos came to visit us and became our friends.

The picture shows what the countryside looked like – it was then virtually unmapped – and, in due course, the small flocks of Ross's Geese flying around the area led us to a major breeding colony. The expedition is described in my book *Wild Geese and Eskimos*.

the way, is achieved by taking a pair of my wife's cast-off tights, rolling them into a ball and using them to dab the paint onto the canvas so as to produce the stippling.) Maybe the commissioner's instructions will make it clear which of these techniques would be most appropriate at the size of picture that has been commissioned.

My pictures have been sold in my own country largely to the shooting fraternity – wildfowlers in particular. They want to be reminded, in the comfort of their homes, of the excitement of their sport. Having been a hunter myself for many years I can easily understand the appeal which leads to this steady demand. But the trouble with such a situation is that it dictates a limited number of subjects – the quarry species of waterfowl – and leads, in the end, to a type of picture in which the birds are not too large nor yet too small, the sky is 'interesting' and the marshy landscape is attractive, while neither is allowed to detract from the quarry. There is room for some artistic creation in the sky and the landscape and in the positioning of the birds to suggest movement, but the upshot is a kind of formula which guarantees sale but limits invention and innovation. It begets a degree of slavery to commissions. 'Will you paint me a picture like the one on page so-and-so of your book *Morning Flight*, only with Canada

Geese instead of Pinkfeet?' If the client is persistent and lucky the picture may be forthcoming within two years, even though it only takes three days to paint. Ideally I like to paint two or three such paintings from which the client may choose. This gives two spare paintings which can go to exhibitions or be acquired directly from my studio.

The critics have only rarely approved of my pictures. I suppose I am too 'square' for them. As you can see in this book my style is such that you know almost at once you have done wrong if you hang one upside-down. As Archbishop Garnett said, 'any fool can criticize and many of them do.'

William Warburton, Bishop of Gloucester, who died in 1779, said, 'orthodoxy is my doxy and heterodoxy is someone else's doxy.' I suppose that I am an orthodox painter. Only once or twice have I explored the realms of allegory or pure abstraction. Some abstract painters seem to me to have something in common with the cross-eyed javelin thrower who was asked what his chances were in the competition. 'I don't know whether I shall win,' he said, 'but at least I should have the attention of the spectators.'

Painting styles differ much with fashion. When photography was invented, artists were suddenly released from the search for verisimilitude, which led in due course to Impressionism and Cubism and all the other 'isms' that have bedeviled artists ever since. These days, however, pictures of birds and mammals which show every feather or every hair seem to be the most admired; and impressionism is, for the time being, rather out of fashion. Ultra-verisimilitude now seems to be in, as it used to be before the invention of colour photography, and artists seem to be trying to outdo the camera.

If beauty is truth and truth beauty, how much freedom is left for the imprint of the artist's individuality? When colour photography was invented, what was left for the bird painter who believed, as I did, that

Brent Geese landing. Date unknown. Black ink. Actual size of drawing.

Mallards coming in from the south. 1979. Oil on canvas. 28 × 36 in.

The title tells you that it is an evening sky; the water and the emergent 'sweet grass' tell you that the wind is from the north-west. If the birds are migrating it must be the spring, and they may have been flying all day. The clouds at high altitude indicate strong winds.

The stippled effect was produced by rolling a pair of discarded tights into a ball and dabbing it onto paint initially added to the canvas with a palette knife.

nature had achieved a perfection that was sacrosanct? Who was I to distort the shapes, to exaggerate the colours, to try to improve on nature? Yet when an artist sets out to paint three-dimensional nature in two dimensions the process of interpretation has begun, and consciously or subconsciously some part of the artist's personality creeps in. There is composition – where and how the shapes and colours should be related to each other. There is economy – what to put in and what to leave out, what must be stated and what left unsaid, what should be underlined, and what merely suggested. And there is always the possibility that 'caricature' can convey a basic truth more succinctly. These are the justifications for artistic licence, in the painter's continuing effort to make pictures that give pleasure to the people who look at them.

Chapter 2 Birds for People

'Plures amicos mensa quam mens concipit.'
(The table attracts more friends than the mind.)

PUBLILIUS SYRUS

Detail from *The East Lighthouse at high tide*. 1961. Oil on canvas. 20 × 24 in.

This was my home in the years immediately before the Second World War. It was at the mouth of the River Nene where it then ran out into the Wash at Sutton Bridge. In those days the lighthouse was surrounded by sea on three sides at high spring tides, and Pink-footed Geese often landed on the saltings nearby. This was a lighthouse built at the end of the eighteenth century, together with its twin on the west side of the river mouth, to commemorate the completion of a final stage in the drainage of the Great Fens, and I lived in it for five years. A single young Pink-footed Goose whom I named Anabel flew in to join the little flock of 'pinioned' Pinkfeet which I kept in a pen by the lighthouse, and thereafter returned each winter. I told the details of the place where I lived and painted, and the story of Anabel, to Paul Gallico, and although he never came there, the story inspired him to write **The Snow Goose**, for which many years later I painted the illustrations, and later still raised Snow Geese to play the part in the television film.

We live on the south side of the estuary of the River Severn at Slimbridge in a house which we built for ourselves 25 years ago, and to which we have added down the years. It is all among the wildfowl, to which I long ago lost my heart. I respond to their beauty, they to the food we offer. The wildfowl are the *raison d'être* of the organization that I founded in 1946 – the Wildfowl Trust. In short, we 'live over the shop'.

Before the Second World War, I lived in a lighthouse on the Wash, where I kept a small collection of tame waterfowl and painted. I had been thinking, both before and during the war, about how I would develop, after it, an organization for research into these birds that excited me so much. But, by the end of the war, the lighthouse was much less attractive than it had been when I lived there, and was for many reasons quite unsuitable for my purpose. New sea walls had been built for land reclamation, so that the salting which had surrounded it was no longer covered by sea at high tide and therefore no longer salting. Instead, the lighthouse was already half a mile inland standing in arable fields. And so in 1945 I was looking for a new place in which to develop my dream of a research station for the study of wildfowl.

In January 1945 I came to the Severn Estuary on a hunch I might find, among the White-fronted Geese which I knew had wintered there from time immemorial, a Lesser White-fronted Goose. The European Whitefronts which winter in Britain come from breeding grounds in northern Siberia, more than 2,000 miles away from the Severn Estuary, whereas the Lessers breed, sparingly, as far west as Scandinavia. At the end of the Second World War, the Lesser White-fronted Goose was the rarest possible British bird. It had only been recorded once, when one was shot on the coast of Northumberland in 1886. To be sure it shared this distinction with about twenty other species recorded only once. During the War a second Lesser was seen in Britain by a farmer friend, Will Tinsley, who lived in Holbeach Marsh on the south shore of the Wash. This bird had come down to the pond in his orchard, and stayed for some weeks with some tame

Lesser Whitefronts which I had kept at the lighthouse, but farmed out to Will when I left to join the Navy.

This second Lesser was an unofficial record, as it was never formally reported and listed by the powers-that-be in the ornithological world. But I was quite satisfied that Will's identification had been correct. I then thought that perhaps occasional Lesser Whitefronts might come regularly to Britain. After all, the differences between the European Whitefront and the Lesser are very small. The Lesser is not quite so large, has a shorter, pinker bill, and a yellow ring round the eye. Knowing how few people in those days looked carefully at wild geese in winter, I wondered how many Lesser White-fronted Geese had come and gone unnoticed.

There was a further factor. If you are a wild goose and you get lost, you find it more comfortable to be among a flock than by yourself, even if the flock belongs to some other species of goose. Thus it is quite common to find stray single geese among larger flocks of another species. If, therefore, you are looking for a stray Lesser Whitefront you should look among flocks of a species whose migration crosses the migration route of the Lessers. The Lessers from Scandinavia head south-eastwards towards eastern Europe and Asia, while the European Whitefronts come west-south-west to us from Russia. The crossing point is probably in Denmark and Holland. To put my theory to the test, it was necessary to visit the largest flock of European Whitefronts in Britain, and this flock winters on the Severn Estuary. So one day in January 1945 I came to look critically at the 2,000 wild geese at Slimbridge, and found two Lesser Whitefronts in different parts of the flock, two lost birds which had not even discovered each other. As well as the Lessers we saw six other species of geese on that day, and as we returned up the muddy lane from the salt marsh, I decided that here was the place in which to establish the new research station which I had been planning for so long.

The Wildfowl Trust began in quite a small way at Slimbridge, but now has seven centres open to the public, up and down the country. Apart from their primary aims of research, education and conservation, the establishment of these centres has given me the additional pleasure of another kind of creative activity – that of making landscapes on the ground instead of on canvas. My first efforts at landscape creation were in digging small ponds to accommodate the collection of captive waterfowl which was one of the elements of the Wildfowl Trust at Slimbridge from its earliest beginnings.

Some time later, when we were able to build a house overlooking one of the enclosures, we included a modest-sized new pond which was dug immediately in front of our windows. This was quite carefully landscaped with islands and trees, and laid out primarily, at that time, for the tame birds which lived in the enclosure. What I did not then know was that the pond, and the food we put round its edges, would attract large numbers of wintering wild birds in the future.

Before that came about, however, His Royal Highness The Duke of Edinburgh became President of the Trust, and agreed to come and stay in our new house. We wondered how to make the evening more

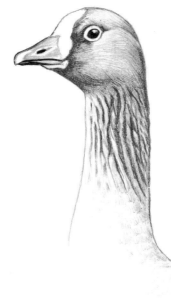

Lesser White-fronted Geese. 1980. Pencil.
About four-fifths of size of drawings.

A Red-breasted Goose flying with the White-fronts at Slimbridge. 1965. Oil on canvas. 20 × 30 in.

Among the White-fronted Geese that come to Slimbridge in thousands each winter from breeding grounds in the Soviet Arctic there are occasional single birds of other goose species which would rather be in an alien flock than not be in a flock at all. Thus down the years seven Red-breasted Geese have been recorded on the Severn Estuary. In 1959 a single Redbreast arrived after a snowfall. I watched it from the Acrow Tower (then in its original position – it has since been moved 200 yards closer to the river). The reflection of the afternoon sunlight on the snow illuminated the undersides of the flying geese and just below them flew a pair of Mallard. Out on the Dumbles was a small herd of Bewick's Swans shining whiter than the snow – some of the earliest to establish a winter tradition at Slimbridge. A few sheep in the Top New Piece and the Long Ground have been leaving tracks in the snow. In the distance on the left is May Hill with its top-knot of trees, and on the right is the Graham Robertson observation tower built on top of the wartime 'pillbox' from which we recorded the second official British occurrence of the Lesser White-fronted Goose on 16 December 1945. Between them is the River Severn.

interesting for him, and decided to install some floodlights shining onto the pond. This proved to be a great success and the birds looked charming outside the window after dark. We did not foresee that some years later we should be visited by large numbers of wild Bewick's Swans, whose floodlit white plumage would be even more impressive against the dark water.

The swans built up in an interesting and, to us, extraordinary way. Before the foundation of the Wildfowl Trust there were virtually no records on the Severn Estuary of this the smallest of our European swans, which migrate each winter to our country from breeding grounds in the Arctic USSR. In 1948 a single male Bewick's Swan arrived to join some Whistling Swans which lived, pinioned, in one of our enclosures. Because at that time we had no Bewick's Swans in our collection we caught this single 'cob', and were later able to acquire a 'pen' for him from the Rotterdam Zoo. This pair, which we called Mr and Mrs Noah, finally, after several years, bred and produced the first Bewick's Swans known to have been hatched in captivity. (Mrs Noah is still alive and well at Slimbridge, and produced one cygnet last summer (1979), aged at least 32.) When they had been breeding for a

Greenland White-fronted Geese at dawn. 1939. Oil on canvas. 20 × 30 in.

I was sure that the White-fronted Geese breeding in West Greenland and wintering in Ireland and the Hebrides were distinguishable from the European Whitefront *Anser albifrons albifrons*. The picture shows a group of Greenland Whitefronts on a low tide rocky islet in Loch Foyle in Northern Ireland, where John Winter and I had taken a gun-punt to confirm that the Whitefronts in Ireland were the same as six brought back alive from Greenland to my lighthouse on the Wash by David Haig Thomas. On the morning depicted the hunch was confirmed. In 1946 Christopher Dalgety and I were able to publish the name and description which formally established scientific recognition of the subspecies *A. a. flavirostris* which had for so long been overlooked by taxonomic ornithologists.

few years they began to attract occasional passing parties of wild Bewick's Swans. Over some fifteen years these parties built up until, by December 1963, from 20 to 30 swans were spending the winter in the neighbourhood. Part of their day was spent in the enclosures with our tame Whistling and Bewick's Swans, but every time visitors walked round, the birds were disturbed and flew out to the estuary. They would also spend part of the day on the salting which here at Slimbridge is known as 'the Dumbles'.

One day at the beginning of 1964 I decided that it might be very interesting to study these wild Bewick's Swans, but for this purpose it would be necessary to persuade them to come to the pond in front of our house where we could keep them under regular observation. This could only be achieved by bringing the tame Bewick's Swans to the lake outside the studio window; and this was done. But the wild Bewick's continued to fly in to the old pens. Then I realized that over in that part of the grounds there were still four of the North American Whistling Swans, which, although they are quite distinguishable to us, are nevertheless only sub-specifically distinct from the Bewick's. They have mostly black bills, and some of the Bewick's were regarding them as attractive prospective mates. The solution was to bring the tame Whistling Swans over to the pond in front of the house as well. On the very next morning the first wild Bewick's Swan settled in front of our window. It was in fact one which had formed a relationship with one of the Whistling Swans, and because it is said that Maud was the name of

Bewick's Swans over the Severn Estuary. 1966. Oil on canvas. 35 × 60 in.

The view is as seen by an eighth swan looking southward. It is the middle of the day and the neap tide is lapping the foot of the sand cliff at the outer edge of the Dumbles; up on the Dumbles grass the White-fronted Geese are feeding. Behind the sea wall at the back of the Dumbles are the grounds of the Wildfowl Trust at Slimbridge. The swans are a pair, with three cygnets of the year and two from a previous year.

one of the painter Whistler's lady friends, the swan was immediately called Maud. On the next day again a single Bewick's Swan landed with our mixed Bewick's and Whistlers, but I immediately noticed that this was not Maud, and I could tell this because it had much more yellow on its bill than Maud. This simple observation was the beginning of a technique for identifying individual Bewick's Swans which has led to a seventeen-years' study of these fascinating 'tundra swans', as they are called by the Soviets.

Being able to identify every individual by the pattern on its bill, which is as variable as human fingerprints but much more obvious, has enabled us to build up a detailed record of some 3,700 swans since Maud which have visited the pond in front of the studio window up to the end of 1979. As I write this I am sitting in a tower which we have added to our house overlooking the pond now inevitably called 'Swan Lake', and there are at this moment more than 220 Bewick's Swans shining brightly against the dark water under the floodlights. It is quarter past five on a December evening.

In the early days the swans came only to be fed during the day, and at night they would flight out to the river. Now that Swan Lake is larger than it used to be – some 150 yards long and about 60 yards wide with ten islands of varying size – the swans have become more and more ready to spend the night roosting there. I find this a very happy circumstance, because it seems to indicate that they have confidence in the place and are content to remain during the dangerous night hours close to our home. This is a proper relationship between man and bird.

Since the Bewick's Swans adopted our man-made pond and turned it into Swan Lake in February 1964, they have given us enormous pleasure and interest each winter. It is not only because they are beautiful, and come from far away Arctic breeding grounds, it is not only that their music is melodious, and that much mystery surrounds their migrations. It is due, I believe, to two special factors – their longevity and their family life.

Mrs Noah, who bred successfully when she was not less than 32 years old, is our oldest captive Bewick's Swan; and these swans normally mate for life and keep their cygnets with them for the first ten months of their lives. These things make their study over a long period particularly rewarding.

When we first began to look at them, I found no difficulty in memorizing the names and patterns of up to 200 swans, and my wife and daughter, Dafila, could do the same. But we were not always at home, and as the study developed various helpers became involved. Their place of work, in the winter months, was in the left-hand corner of our great studio window. At this later period, Dafila, who had begun to look at them carefully when she was only eleven years old, was carrying up to 1,000 names and faces in her head, and I had forgotten all but a very few. However, I can discover who some of them are by reading their ring numbers through a telescope, for we have been able to catch and ring just over 1,000 Bewick's Swans in a specially constructed 'swan pipe' at the side of our window – a channel 100 yards long covered by netting which leads to a large cage.

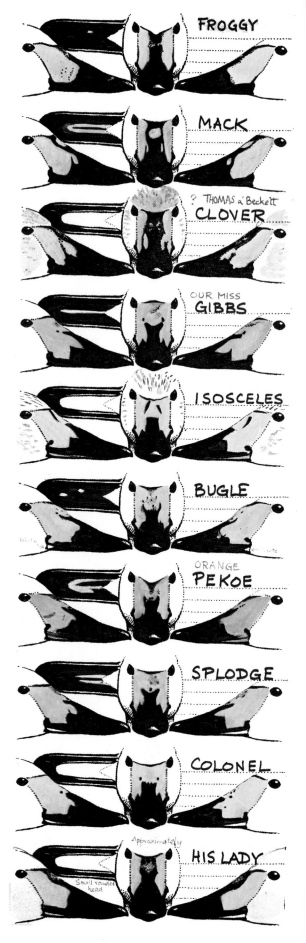

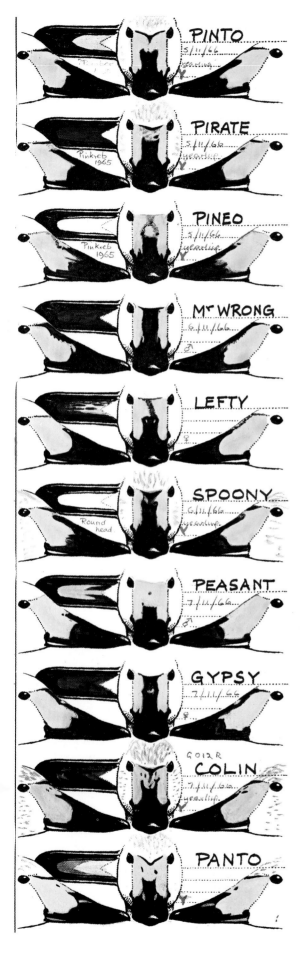

PINTO
5/11/66
yearling

PIRATE
5/11/66
yearling

PINEO
5/11/66
yearling

Mr WRONG
6/11/66

LEFTY

SPOONY
6/11/66
yearling

PEASANT
7/11/66

GYPSY
7/11/66

COLIN
7/11/66
yearling

PANTO

Above: *Peasant and Gypsy with their cygnet.* 1968. Oil on canvas. 12 × 10 in.

Peasant first came to Swan Lake at Slimbridge in 1965. He had a mate whom we called Poet, and two cygnets. In 1966 he came with a new mate, Gypsy. They became one of the favourite pairs of our daughter Dafila, and, as a Christmas present, I painted a picture of them with their single cygnet in 1968. When they arrived they were heavily stained with iron. In 1969 they had no cygnet; but for the next six winters they brought young every year.

Altogether Peasant came to Slimbridge for 12 winters (Gypsy only 11) and brought 15 cygnets. They were last sighted on 24 January 1977, and may yet reappear.

Left: *Bill patterns of Bewick's Swans.* 1966. Ink and watercolour. Each 13 × 4 in.

When they first came onto the pond in front of the studio window, in the winter of 1963–4, we quickly realized that the patterns of black and yellow on Bewick's Swans' bills were infinitely variable. By drawing them in front and side view we could record the different patterns and give each swan a number and a name. We have now recorded the face patterns and given names to more than 3,700 Bewick's Swans.

A very special moment, for me, comes each evening between 6.30 and 7.00 p.m., when we feed the swans from the bins at either end of the studio window. Philippa normally does one end and I the other. It is a dramatic sight as we walk to the windows, because the swans swim in from all over the pond and cluster in a great mass in the brightest part of the lights in front of us. We step out of the end window with a scoop and throw out wheat which splashes first into the water, but later onto the birds' backs as they cluster in the shallows. In front of us no more than six feet away is a solid mass of birds – Bewick's Swans, with a few Mutes, Greylag and Canada Geese (both feral, meaning that they are semi-tame) and quantities of ducks – Tufted, Pochard, Pintail, Shoveler, Mallard and Gadwall. The scene is all movement, picked out crisply by the floodlights – more than 300 of our wildfowl friends within ten yards of us – friends who know us well by sight as individual humans whom they can trust not to be predators.

Below: *Bewick's Swans in a fresh wind.* 1965. Oil on canvas. 25 × 36 in.

The birds were flying low over the water on a rather wild afternoon, and I was interested in white birds against the light, and a sky that complemented their long necks. As I so often have, I believe I made their necks a trifle too long and their heads a trifle too big. The difficulty is to see these things before the picture leaves the studio.

Above: *Bewick's Swans before the storm*. 1967.
Oil on board. 9 × 16 in.

The sun shines on the swans, which include a family of four cygnets, as they sweep in over the flood water of the Tack Piece at Slimbridge against the row of fine trees that stood there until Dutch elm disease killed them all.

Right: *Bewick's Swans in a sunny sky*. 1970. Oil on canvas. 18 × 15 in.

Sometimes swans arrive on Swan Lake at Slimbridge at midday, perhaps after a migratory flight. They fly over first to see that all is clear, then they circle round and come in much lower. If there is another group coming in high the spectator is treated to a most exciting kaleidoscope effect as the directions of movement cross. It is difficult to describe it in words but my intention was to explain it in paint.

Above: *Domestic difficulties – Ruddy Ducks*. 1954. Oil on canvas. About 20 × 30 in.

Two extraneous males displaying to a mother of six, who gets no protection from her mate. In the early days of the Wildfowl Trust some Ruddy Ducks were imported from the United States and soon began to breed.

Ruddy Ducks usually nest close to the water and, if the eggs are taken for artificial incubation, the results we have found are rather unsatisfactory. It is more effective to allow the mother bird to incubate the eggs herself. If, however, the hatching date has not been carefully anticipated, there is some chance that the young birds will jump into the water, after which their diving abilities are such that it is quite impossible to catch them for pinioning one wing so as to prevent them from flying away.

Thus it was that over many years a few Ruddy Ducks escaped from Slimbridge. At first they were recorded breeding on nearby gravel pits, then on reservoirs in the West Country and the Midlands. By 1976 the winter flock of Ruddies on Belvide Reservoir in the Midlands was over 400, and at the same time there were 120 on Chew Valley Lake.

Mindful of the unexpected side effects of introducing such species as the mink and the grey squirrel in Europe, and the rabbit in Australia, the scientific world has roundly condemned all introductions of exotic species into Britain. However, it seems doubtful to me that the Ruddies will ever become a pest or drive out any other species. Like the Mandarin Duck, they will, I believe, prove a harmless and attractive addition to the British avifauna.

Opposite: *Shovelers*. 1957. Oil on canvas. 18 × 14 in.

This is the spelling used by Thomas Bewick, who gave alternative names: Kertlutock or Broadbill. The first may well be taken from the loud drumming noise made by the drakes as they take off, or alternatively perhaps from the double clucking call they make during display.

Bewick's **British Birds** was published in 1804, at which time he wrote, 'It has not yet been ascertained whether the Shoveler breeds in England, where indeed it is a scarce bird; but according to M. Baillon they are not uncommon in France, where they arrive about the month of February, disperse in the marshes, and a part of them hatch every year. He conjectures that they advance southward, for they are seldom met with after the first northerly wind that blows in March, and he adds that those of them which then stay behind do not depart until September.'

It is of course now known that Shovelers advance northward in the spring; but in those days they did not have much to help them elucidate the mysteries of migration.

Pintails in the sun. 1951. Oil on canvas. 15 × 18 in.

After a courtship flight in which the duck has been chased by a number of drakes, the party picks its way down onto the pond through the reed heads. Similar courtship flights take place in most species of 'dabbling ducks', and the main ploy of the female is to escape by flying more slowly than the males. Sometimes duck Pintails are pursued by as many as ten drakes.

Sketches of Mallards. Date unknown. Blue ink on the back of an old manila file. 14 × 9 in.

At bottom left appears a sketch map of part of the shore of Loch Leven, Tayside, now the site of a Royal Society for the Protection of Birds reserve.

There is more to designing a habitat for waterfowl, with facilities for people to watch them without disturbing them, than merely laying out attractive ponds. One has to bear in mind that most people watch birds in the afternoon, and that bird-watching is more effective if the light is behind the viewer. Thus the position of an observatory or a hide for watching wild birds should if possible be in the sector between south and west of the place where the birds are most likely to concentrate. Then there is the question of how the hides are to be approached by the bird-watcher. It is particularly disappointing to see, as you approach a hide, all the birds in the immediate vicinity rising up and flying away. This inevitably happens unless the approach is totally screened, and total screening is a difficult and expensive business.

There is no doubt that the most permanent and most effective screen is an eight-foot bank. This requires little maintenance and can be planted up with shrubs so as to become quite unobtrusive in the landscape. The second best is a wall either of concrete panels or breeze blocks or bricks. Such a wall may well be unacceptable in the land-

FALCON TOWER — P.S.

Black ink. 1980. Actual size of drawing.

Two pairs of Pintails on a bright morning after snow. 1951. Oil on canvas. $17\frac{1}{2} \times 14\frac{1}{2}$ in.

A few feathers fall out after vigorous preening, and on a still day they may float for a little while. I have always thought Pintails extraordinarily beautiful, and I particularly enjoy painting them. Linnaeus placed the bird in the genus *Anas*; but in 1824 an ornithologist named Stephens decided that the Pintail rated a genus of its own, and he called it **Dafila acuta**. It appears that he invented the name Dafila as the most elegant name he could think of for the most elegant duck he knew. And then in 1923 John Phillips, who was writing his great monograph *The Natural History of the Ducks*, decided to lump some of these new genera back into the genus *Anas*. Dafila became obsolete.

When our daughter was born, Philippa and I decided to revive the name Dafila by giving it to her. Only recently she was saying that she was quite pleased with the name because there were not many other Dafilas around.

scape, but it can be hidden by shrubs and is relatively maintenance-free. After that come screens either of wood or of reeds or of straw which do not last long, but can be effective in a temporary situation when more expensive screening is financially ruled out. Finally, by far the cheapest is a hedge; but these are usually rather unsatisfactory, because they take time to establish themselves, and inevitably there are holes and gaps through which the birds will see the approaching watcher.

And what of the hides themselves? The Wildfowl Trust has detailed drawings of the latest designs which have proved to be the most effective, and it is surprising how many hides have been and are still being built by well-meaning people, without taking advantage of our 34 years of experience. For example, the rather narrow horizontal shutter in front of the hide should have its middle line at the eye level of the average seated viewer. It should be hinged at the *bottom*, and the top edge should leave a half-inch gap. On entering, the watcher can apply his eye to the crack by stretching up a little, and can easily see whether there are birds so near that they will be disturbed by any movement of the shutter. When it is opened, the crack can be controlled at any width by having a chain on which it can be hooked, and the shutter itself then acts as a rest for binoculars as well. If the shutter is hinged at the top, none of these advantages can be obtained – yet shutters hinged at the top are still fitted to new bird-watchers' hides.

The design of the hides themselves is of vital importance not only in their internal dimensions but in their external appearance. On this subject there are two schools of thought: one is to try to conceal the hide so meticulously that the casual viewer would not even notice it was there. Another is to make a reasonably attractive small building which fits the landscape. From the point of view of the birds it makes absolutely no difference. They are prepared to accept the presence of a man-made object provided they are adequately accustomed to it. The Wildfowl Trust has developed both these types of hides.

The exact siting of a hide is of great importance, and often it is possible to give a better view by adding height to the viewing point. This has led to the development, at some of our seven Wildfowl Trust centres, of 'watch-towers' overlooking wide areas.

I have been active at the design stage of most of these towers. The principal monuments to my architectural creativity are the Holden Tower, the House Tower, the Gazebo and the Pagoda, all at Slimbridge, the observatory and the House Tower at Eastpark, Caerlaverock, and the observatory at Welney. I have to admit that my input in each case was not much more than a few sketches which were then converted either by local architects or directly by the builders. But it does not diminish my architectural pride when I look at these rather quaint structures.

Falcon Tower is in a different category. It provides the highest overlook at Slimbridge – 47 feet from its topmost vantage point. And in this case our son Falcon can claim the sole credit for the whole operation, having designed and built it entirely himself. In concept

and execution it was a one-man project which extended over several years, starting in his school days.

Back in the 1930s I visited a beautiful place in Canada called Cap Tourmente at the mouth of the St Lawrence River. The little hunting lodge in which we stayed had a huge picture window overlooking the marsh, and one day several thousand Greater Snow Geese began to feed up towards the lodge. I remember being amazed at how close they came to the building, and also being delighted by the way in which the window made a frame for the living scene outside. The view which to me was enthralling was somehow enhanced by the fact that it was seen through a window. So when we built our house at Slimbridge it had a picture window looking out over birds. And I found, almost to my surprise, that many other people thought a window frame added to the beauty of a crowd of living birds – it was not merely the foible of an artist conditioned by the frames which were essential to his own trade.

We are, of course, not the first to think that way. For centuries people have been designing their gardens so that they look beautiful through the frame of their window. In the case of the Wildfowl Trust, the ponds which create the spectacle of birds have been developed as jumbo bird tables.

So the Slimbridge window originated in concept at Cap Tourmente in Canada; it was then seen by those who were to build the Laboratory of Ornithology at Cornell University in the USA. They improved on the idea by making two such windows in their entrance hall, because they had more people to accommodate than could look through one frame. And the two-window idea came back across the Atlantic to be incorporated in the new entrance building that was being designed for Slimbridge. Since then picture windows have been the order of the day at all Wildfowl Trust centres – Peakirk, Welney, Caerlaverock, Martin Mere, Washington and Arundel.

Snow Geese and a Blue Goose. 1937. Oil on canvas. 36 × 96 in.

This picture, a yard deep and nearly three yards long, was painted for the Summer Exhibition at the Royal Academy to occupy a high site far above the pictures on the famous 'line'.

The single Blue Goose is a colour morph of the Lesser Snow Goose. This flock is fairly far west in the North American range of the species, probably in the Pacific Flyway.

October dusk – Mallards. 1945. Oil on canvas. About 20 × 30 in.

The Mallards are coming in to a flooded marsh where the willows have not yet lost their leaves, and the reeds have not yet dropped their seeds. But there will be plenty of food for them on the newly inundated land. This was painted at the end of the war, when I wanted to make peaceful unambitious pictures that were restful to look at.

For 34 years now, the Wildfowl Trust seems to have been operating on a perpetual shoestring. We have used phrases like 'when our ship comes home' and 'when someone gives us a million'. We dream hopefully of a time when the Trust will be 'rich beyond the dreams of aviaries' . . . But on the other hand we have been wonderfully lucky to have so many friends and members who have supported us loyally down the years. Some of them have been quite unbelievably generous, and without their help we could not possibly have developed the Wildfowl Trust as we have.

Our first branch was at Peakirk in what was then Northamptonshire and has now become Cambridgeshire, quite close to the famous duck decoy at Borough Fen, that was operated for nearly 300 years by the Williams family.

I had known the Williamses and the decoy since 1932, and many of my early pictures were painted there. In those days the ducks were caught for the market. But in 1956 the Wildfowl Trust became tenants, and from then on the decoyman, Billy Williams, ringed the ducks' legs instead of wringing their necks.

In order to pay, we hoped, for the upkeep of this ancient eight-pipe decoy, we set up a collection of tame waterfowl – a mini-Slimbridge – at Peakirk two miles from the decoy. It was a small, sparsely wooded area of considerable charm which had to be landscaped into ponds and paths and bridges, and when the birds were added it was delightful.

A few years after that, one of our council members, Vincent Weir, called me on the telephone and asked whether the Trust would be interested in acquiring some land in the Ouse Washes near Welney, because if so he would buy 100 acres of these water meadows and present them to the Trust. The price was £40 per acre and the year 1967. I think I said 'snap' there and then, or words to that effect, and that was the beginning of the Welney Wildfowl Refuge – the Trust's third centre.

In olden times the River Great Ouse meandered in a huge loop through the fenlands of East Anglia. At one stage in the drainage planning of the seventeenth century it was decided that there should be a kind of short cut dug across the loop, to take the water away to the sea more quickly. As the new drainage dried the land, it sank down so that in the end it was many feet below sea level. It was necessary for the water to be pumped up into the embanked river system – much of it into the short-cut river; but it was realized that at flood times the water load would be too great for a river of ordinary width to carry, and so

Opposite: *'Swan Fall' at Welney.* 1973. Oil on canvas. 25 × 30 in.

Like a fall of snow, a fall of Bewick's Swans arrives at the Welney Refuge of the Wildfowl Trust on the famous Ouse Washes in the west Norfolk fens. At Welney the Washes (each field is a 'wash', and the water runs out into 'The Wash') are half a mile wide, and at times of high flood they become an inland sea. But at half flood they attract huge numbers of water birds. More than 30,000 Wigeon, many thousands of other ducks, and up to 2,000 wild swans can be seen from the Trust's observatory. The swans are fed in the lagoon, which has become a kind of bird table on a vast scale outside the observatory windows. Here, as at Slimbridge, scientific studies of Bewick's Swan behaviour have been pursued, based on the recognition of individual birds. It was from this observatory that most of my daughter Dafila's work was carried out in obtaining her Doctor's degree. So many people came to see the birds from the observatory that since the picture was painted it has become necessary to build wings on either side of the central observation room. Now 200 people can watch the birds at the same time.

Left: *A courting party of Smews.* 1966. Oil on canvas. 15 × 18 in.

Adult drake Smews are much less frequently seen in winter in Britain than the brown-headed immatures, but recently we had a distant view of an adult pair from the main observatory at Welney. In courtship the female has a delightful nodding display with down-turned bill, and the male raises the front part of his crest while depressing the feathers on the nape. At an earlier stage of the display, shown by the farthest drake, the crest at the back of the head is raised.

Even at the beginning of the nineteenth century, ornithologists were confused about the Smew. Bewick called the adult male 'the Smew or White Nun', the female was 'the Red-headed Smew or Weesel Coot,' and the immatures were 'the Lough-diver.'

Of the Lough-diver Bewick writes: 'In describing this as the female Smew, Mr Pennant says it has "around the eyes a spot of the same colour and form as in the

male"; he afterwards corrects his error in supposing it the female and adds "The bird I had thought to be the female and called the Lough-diver, is a distinct kind." Mr Plymley informs me that he dissected several and found males and females without any distinction of plumage in either sex.'

I suspect that even in these days it is no less alarmingly easy to reach false conclusions in science.

another parallel bank was built about half a mile north-west of the river, in order that the strip of land between could act as a kind of safety-valve. This constitutes the Ouse Washes, which run for 22 miles from Earith Bridge to Denver Sluice, diagonally from south-west to north-east across the Great Fens.

At some times during most winters the Ouse Washes are totally flooded; but for much of the winter they are only partially so, and make a perfect habitat for water birds. This, then, is the area in which the Wildfowl Trust's Welney Refuge has been established. It now consists of more than 800 acres of prime wetland habitat.

As soon as we had enough land to make a viable sanctuary, the wildfowl began to concentrate in it, especially on Saturdays when there was shooting on many other parts of the Ouse Washes. And we have been able to flood artificially certain fields in front of our main observatory and our observation hides. This is particularly effective when there is no other flood water out on the washes.

The result has been that huge numbers of ducks have from time to time assembled there – huge numbers, that is to say, for this country. In some winters we have had more than 35,000 Wigeon on the sanctuary, and the Bewick's Swans, with some Whooper Swans among them, have taken to roosting most nights on the lagoon that we have laid out in front of the observatory. Often more than a thousand Bewick's Swans can be seen there lit up by the floodlights we have installed.

Recently we have built a 'swan pipe' so as to catch and ring some of the Welney swans. It is a kind of trap, similar to the one we have used successfully for seven years on Swan Lake at Slimbridge, in which we had caught 1,000 Bewick's by 1979. At Welney it will be specially interesting to find out from ringing where our Whooper Swans breed. The answer could be Scandinavia or the USSR, or they may be part of the Icelandic breeding population. At present we have no real idea which, though we favour the Scandinavian/Russian theory.

Wigeon in a popple. 1957. Oil on canvas. 25 × 30 in.

A flock of Wigeon lit from behind by the early morning sun. To me the most delightful things about Wigeon are the whistle of the drake and their gregarious habits. Great flocks of Wigeon such as we see on the flooded Ouse Washes at Welney (once 35,000 together) or on the Dumbles at Slimbridge, or at Martin Mere – or even the few hundred outside the observatory at Eastpark, Caerlaverock – always stir my imagination. Their glorious high pitched 'whee-you' takes me back to the spring tides that came over the saltings at night round my lighthouse long ago. And this year, one morning, there were almost 5,000 Wigeon among the White-fronted Geese on the Tack Piece within earshot of my new tower at Slimbridge.

Peter Scott 1957

Wigeon at dusk on Chew Valley Lake. 1975. Oil on board. 28 × 36 in.

This large reservoir south of Bristol was built by its water authority, which tackled the problem of competing leisure interests with consummate skill and foresight. It supports a flourishing sailing club, which operates within a strictly regulated area, and also makes provision for fishermen. A large secluded area remains an ornithologist's delight, carrying large numbers of birds, especially waterfowl.

This painting was one of several submitted for a commission, and was subsequently used for the dust jacket of a revised edition of my autobiography, published in 1977.

We have built banks in various parts of the Welney Wildfowl Refuge, so that people can walk along screened approaches to our hides, and I know of few things more exciting than to creep up behind these banks into a hide and look out across the marsh. To give you an example of a recent visit, we had walked over the screened footbridge to the observatory to watch the morning flight. Ducks were moving everywhere, low over the marsh, and the swans began flighting out to the fields to eat the waste potatoes which had been softened by recent frosts. Taking off from the water in front of us, they flew in small parties often close past the observatory windows and sometimes directly overhead. After a while the ducks began rising away to our right – hundreds at a time, mostly Wigeon. Wave after wave got up, and I was looking in vain for the slow flapping and gliding flight of a Marsh Harrier that had been seen there during the last few days. Then suddenly the panic was over and the birds were landing back peacefully. Max Williams, the Trust's honorary treasurer, was looking through the huge German military binocular telescope ('liberated' at the end of the war and presented to the Trust by the Army), when he suddenly stopped their swing and said, 'I think I've found a Peregrine.' There, no more than 200 yards away, a small dark Peregrine tiercel was standing on a still-moving drake Teal, which he proceeded to kill, pluck and eat as we watched. Even though we had not seen the stoop, it was as good a view of a wild Peregrine as we could wish.

Leaving the observatory, we walked along behind the high screen bank, on which we have planted willows to increase the cover, and came up into each of the small fibreglass hides that are spaced along it every few hundred yards. In front of almost every hide were Wigeon, Teal and Tufted Ducks, sometimes only a few yards away. One area has been specially designed to provide feeding places for waders, and here we were lucky. As well as dozens of Snipe, some feeding extremely close to us, we saw large numbers of Lapwings, some Golden Plover, one or two Ringed Plover, quantities of Redshanks, at least a score of Ruffs and one late Black-tailed Godwit. This elegant species chose to re-establish itself as a breeding bird on the Ouse Washes at the end of the Second World War after an absence of more than 100 years.

The observatory at Welney holds about 30 bird-watchers in reasonable comfort; it is carpeted to prevent noise and heated to make winter watching more bearable. But we have had to build less luxurious extensions on either side of it to increase the capacity to 200 people – and still on occasions it is full. The central room is now reserved for Wildfowl Trust members.

Welney's popularity is heartening in several ways. It means that the Trust will have enough money to keep the place running. But much more important, it means that ever increasing numbers of people are being exposed to what Lord Grey of Fallodon described in the title of his best book as 'The Charm of Birds'.

In my University days, at Christmas time 1928 we went to the north shore of the Solway Firth for a wildfowling holiday. It was the beginning of my love affair with a stretch of Scottish coastline between the River Nith and the Lochar Water, which includes the ruined castle of Caerlaverock (the Castle of the Lark), the site of the fourth Wildfowl Trust centre to be established. The huge expanses of sand and the lawn-like 'merses', covered by the high spring tides, are the wintering grounds of Barnacle Geese, and in those days also of Greylag Geese, nowadays largely replaced by Pink-footed Geese, especially in early spring.

The area is dominated to the west by the elegant outline of Criffel, 1,866 feet high, and to the north by lower hills, the nearest to the Solway being the Ward Law, crowned by a circular clump of trees – the Worley Wood. It is a most compelling landscape.

Between the merse and the hill there are arable fields, and at the eastern end, next to the Lochar and at the extremity of the road, is a farm called Eastpark, consisting of 200 acres of arable land and 600 acres of merse. In those days and for more than 40 years thereafter it was part of the estate of Bernard, 16th Duke of Norfolk.

Peregrine Falcon. Date unknown. Black ink. About two-thirds of size of drawing.

Snipe. Date unknown. Black ink. Actual size of drawing.

The Pinkfeet followed the line of the creek and landed on the south side. 1975. Oil on canvas. 15 × 18 in.

The title is an elaborate way of explaining that we are looking to the east, and therefore it is dawn rather than dusk. And the geese are swinging round in the air to land with the little party they have only just seen on the salting. Meanwhile by chance the Wigeon are crossing to the south side of the creek too.

This area was, and still is, the only wintering ground for Barnacle Geese on the mainland of Scotland. But the geese got little peace. Wildfowlers were after them on the merse and the farmers used 'bangers' to scare them from the arable fields. After the war the Barnacles had been reduced to less than 500, whereas in the 1930s there had been several thousand. 'If Eastpark ever becomes vacant,' I once said to the Duke, 'I should dearly like to become the tenant, or maybe it could be taken over by the Wildfowl Trust.'

Bernard's great interest in wildfowl led him to accept the Presidency of the Trust in succession to the Duke of Edinburgh in 1968. And then in 1970 the farm became available and the Wildfowl Trust acquired a long lease.

Four things had to be done. First we needed hides. Next we needed screen-banks so that people could reach the hides unseen by the geese. Third we needed some ponds and a fox-proof fence in order to establish a small collection of native wildfowl species, to act as decoys to draw the wild ones into an area close to our proposed new observatory, which would also be an education centre. And finally we had to find the money for all this.

Furthermore, although wild swans were then a rarity in the area, we wanted to develop a new place for them, using the experience gained from Swan Lake at Slimbridge. To do this it would be necessary to keep a few pairs of tame ones on the ponds, in order to call in the wild ones when they passed. The most likely swans to respond to this were Whooper Swans, belonging we believe to the Icelandic, rather than the Scandinavian or Russian, breeding populations, though again we have no proof yet. Already on the west side of the Nith there was a wintering Whooper group that was sometimes in excess of 100. We hoped to draw some of them over to Eastpark without difficulty.

But the most important job was to build up the failing Barnacle population, which we discovered consisted of the entire breeding output of Spitsbergen. Two other Barnacle breeding areas are East Greenland and Novaya Zemlya north of the USSR. The strange part is that these three populations appear to keep themselves to themselves. The Greenland birds, at present some 20,000 to 25,000 strong, winter in the Western Isles of Scotland, and in Ireland – the Inner Hebridean island of Islay being their principal stronghold. The Russian birds – perhaps 35,000 strong – winter in Denmark and Holland. And the Spitsbergen birds, in the middle, come down the Norwegian coast, cross the North Sea and the Scottish mainland to winter apparently almost exclusively on the Solway Firth, and it seems that there is hardly any interchange of individuals between the three groups, even though Eastpark, Caerlaverock, is barely 100 miles from Islay.

Pink-footed Goose. Date unknown. Black ink. About four-fifths of size of drawing.

View from the window at Eastpark, Caerlaverock – Pinkfeet, Wigeon and Pintails. 1975. Oil on canvas. 24 × 24 in.

From the observation room that we built on to Eastpark farmhouse, you can look out on to a pond with islands that I designed in the grass field just outside. In March and April, the Barnacle Geese who use the field on and off all winter often move up the Solway to Rockcliffe Marsh. But then their place is taken by up to a thousand or more Pink-footed Geese. The open Solway is beyond the dunes known as the Salcot Hills, with their benchmark on the skyline, and the lone sycamore leans from the westerly wind. If the day had been much clearer, we should have seen the distant hills of the Lake District across the firth.

Barnacle Geese in flight. Date unknown. Black ink. About four-fifths of size of drawing.

Barnacles disturbed. 1937. Oil on canvas. 15 × 18 in.

One of my earliest pictures of the Solway scene with Criffel in the background and the Worley Wood on the extreme right. The whins of the Long Ridden were less extensive in those days than the large area of gorse bushes that grow on the Eastpark merse today. But the main point is that the Barnacle Geese are still there, and in even bigger numbers than they were in the days before the war.

A few years before the Wildfowl Trust took over Eastpark, the Nature Conservancy under the leadership of Max Nicholson had concluded an agreement with the Duke to create a National Nature Reserve covering the merse and the sand all the way from the Nith to the Lochar. The central third of the long strip of merse was to be a controlled shooting area requiring a special permit, and the western third would remain the private shooting ground of the estate. Only the eastern end, of which Eastpark had the grazing, was to be a full sanctuary. This is the regime which remains to this day. At the time, the concept of a shooting area within a Nature Reserve was quite new.

It is still obscure what caused the numbers of Spitsbergen Barnacles to turn the corner, for there seems to have been a modest increase even before the effects of the new Reserve could have been expected to show. However, both the setting up of the Reserve and the total protection of the Solway Barnacles undoubtedly helped; and the birds began to increase again. By 1962 there were 3,000; by 1968 they had

The white Barnacle at Caerlaverock. 1971. Oil on canvas. 28 × 36 in.

In March 1935 there were 4,000 Barnacle Geese at Caerlaverock, including a single leucistic bird (white, but without the pink eyes of a true albino). I tried to catch that white bird with some spring nets I had invented; but they didn't go off properly, and I only caught two normal birds.

In 1971 there was a single white bird in the flock, here seen against the dark hillside of Criffel; but in subsequent years up to four appeared. The Wildfowl Trust scientists, studying the Barnacles on their breeding grounds, managed to catch and ring three of them. In due course two disappeared; but in 1979 a young white bird brought the number up again.

The sycamore tree at Eastpark. 1974. Oil on canvas. 20 × 30 in.

In 1974 the flock at Caerlaverock contained four white Barnacle Geese – leucistic mutants – which may be picked out among the feeding birds. The lone windswept sycamore tree stands at the side of a grass field which is a favourite for the Barnacles; and they can often be watched from one of the Trust's hides along the west side of the Salcot Lane.

Barnacle Goose. Date unknown. Black ink. About four-fifths of size of drawing.

increased to over 4,000; then there was an upward turn between 1970 and 1976; and by 1978 there were 8,800, though in 1979 they had dropped back to 7,700.

To creep into one of the hides at Eastpark when the Barnacles are close in front of it is unforgettably exciting. The milling mass of black and white and grey, the carpet of intricate pattern, the chatter of the feeding flock, the very closeness of these very wary wild birds, add up to a singular and memorable experience. Anyone who goes to Eastpark in the winter should also spend some time sitting in the observatory. The view from there can be enchanting. Already the wintering Whooper Swans have built up to a peak of over 100, although surprisingly this does not seem to have in any way diminished the numbers frequenting the marshes of the lower Nith at Isle Steps.

The Whooper Pond, and the House Pond on the other side of Eastpark Farm House, are, like Swan Lake at Slimbridge and the observatory areas of all the Trust's centres, massive bird tables. Whereas the Barnacles are mainly attracted by good grass and freedom from disturbance, the swans and many of the ducks respond to the grain which is put out for them from a wheelbarrow. Food, as we have discovered, is always the way to a bird's heart, and the principle applies to most animals, particularly vegetarians (herbivores) which must spend so much of their lives eating.

Martin Mere lies to the east of Southport in Lancashire. It was an ancient shallow lake of several thousand acres that had been almost totally drained. No open water whatever remained, but a small area was so difficult to drain that it had remained grassland, instead of the valuable black peaty arable of the rest of the former lake. In 1972 the Trust bought 364 acres of this grass and turned it back into wetland, digging a lake of 20 acres which, as the only permanent water in the area, could rightly be once more designated Martin Mere. Next door to it were two areas of marsh that could be flooded at will.

For many years the nearby potato fields have been winter feeding grounds for many thousands of Pink-footed Geese, and it was my hope that these could be persuaded to use our new mere and its surrounding floods as a place to roost on at night and to flight to by day for a drink. In fact Martin Mere has attracted birds and people in astonishing numbers. At times the counts of both Pintail and Teal have exceeded 6,000, and once there were no fewer than 14,000 Pinkfeet in the Plover Field. In the winter of 1979/80 several thousand Pinkfeet have been roosting on the mere, and the Bewick's and Whooper Swans have begun to build up.

Further to the north and east is the Washington Waterfowl Park between Newcastle and Sunderland. We were offered 100 acres which were a part of the Washington New Town Development Corporation's land. Its Chairman, Sir James Steel, was a keen ornithologist and asked us whether we could create another Slimbridge in the North-East. The main problem, however, was that it was not a flat marshy area, but rather a shallow valley on the north side of the River Wear, and the only way to make ponds was to dig them round the

Pintails often came to the little marsh by the twin elm trees. 1968. Oil on board. 9 × 16 in.

I expect they still do; but the twins are there no more, since the elm disease struck.

In this picture the heads of the **Phragmites** reeds have been used to knit the composition together, and the branches of the static trees are more crisply in focus than the moving ducks.

Shelducks in morning mist. 1975. Oil on canvas. $21\frac{1}{2} \times 25$ in.

The bird's name is derived from the Saxon word 'sheld', meaning pied.

The technique of painting the birds so that they recede into the mist presents an agreeable challenge, and I have been drawn to it a number of times.

Shelducks are usually maritime birds. But surprisingly they breed in two of the Trust's inland reserves – at Martin Mere, which is about 4 miles from the Ribble estuary, and at Welney, which is 17 miles from the Wash.

contours of the hill, like rice paddies. There is a good collection of wildfowl which breed well in captivity. The accent is on North American species because George Washington's family came from there; so it is a place of pilgrimage to many Americans. There is also a wild area called 'Wader Lake', down beside the river, which attracts a number of unusual waders and other passage migrants every year.

Our reserve at Arundel in Sussex is a gem. With only 70 acres of land we have managed to lay out an excellent collection area and a small but very rich wild area with a wader scrape. The Visitor Centre has a vista of Arundel Castle, reflected in Swan Lake. The Bewick's Swans, about 100 of which winter each year on Amberley Wildbrooks, have not so far been persuaded by our tame Bewick's to land in our reserve, though in due course I am sure they will.

Peter Scott
1968

Chapter 3   Concern for the Planet

'Architects cover their mistakes with creepers, cooks with sauces, doctors with earth.'

OLD PORTUGUESE PROVERB

'Man covers the earth with his mistakes.'

MY UPDATING

Indian fauna. 1968. Black ink. $9\frac{3}{4} \times 7\frac{3}{4}$ in.

The animals illustrated are: Chinkara Gazelle (top left), overlapped by Markhor; Great Indian Bustard (top right); Black Buck (centre right); Indian Tiger; Snow Leopard; Western Tragopan.

Art and science, or perhaps science and art (for that was the order in which I was trained in the two activities), have been twin pre-occupations all my life; and the furtherance of scientific research has always been one of the Wildfowl Trust's prime objectives. However, research was not the only consideration I had in mind for Slimbridge. There was also education, and I had for long been concerned about conservation – concerned for the prospects of survival of many of the wildfowl species in a hostile world. And I was anxious not only about the wildfowl, for it was clear that all over the world a great number of other animal species – and plant species too – were threatened with extinction. These species were the current end-products of 40 million centuries of evolution – four billion years. This is how long it has taken for all the diversity of living creatures on our earth to evolve into what we know today; and, of course, the process is continuing.

For me one of the greatest fascinations in nature is the way that evolution has produced this diversity of species moulded by the particular environment they live in. Their study leads me to value each evolutionary creation, each species, very highly, and to look upon species extinction at the hands of unthinking man – sometimes even by his deliberate choice – as wicked irresponsibility. Extinction is for ever. It is irrevocable, irreversible. We have a responsibility to prevent species extinction if it is in our power to do so.

These principles I expressed in a book called *Wild Chorus*, published in 1938. I drew attention to the impending extinction of the Nene or Hawaiian Goose. The story of how, in the 1950s, the Wildfowl Trust was able to take part in a restoration plan, breeding large numbers of the birds in captivity at Slimbridge, has been told elsewhere. From three original birds sent by the late Herbert Shipman from Hawaii, and four males sent subsequently for fresh blood, over a thousand birds were raised in the next thirty years, and 200 were sent over to repopulate the Haleakala Crater on the Island of Maui.

Nenes on the slope of Mauna Loa. 1965. Oil on board. 48 × 96 in.

By 1949 there were believed to be no more than 42 Nenes (or Hawaiian Geese) alive in the world. Thirty of them were in captivity – the property of Herbert Shipman, who did more than anyone else to save the species from extinction. At that time the Curator of the three-year-old Wildfowl Trust was John Yealland, who went to Hawaii to demonstrate captive breeding techniques which we hoped might help their sur-

vival. When he returned he brought a 'pair' for Slimbridge; but they turned out to be two females, and in the spring they both laid eggs, which of course were infertile. We blew the eggs, ate the contents in an omelette, and cabled for a male to be sent from Hawaii. He arrived one week later; but he was in moult, and the second clutches of the two females were also infertile. In the following season he bred with both of them, and the population began to build up at Slimbridge. Much later we twice received two new males from

Hawaii – bringing the total sent to us up to 7 birds. From these, by 1979, 1,200 had been produced and 200 had been sent to repopulate the Haleakala Crater on the island of Maui, where the species had formerly been recorded, but was extinct.

In the picture, a flock of Nenes is about to land at the edge of a kipuka (an island of vegetation in a more recent lava flow) on the eastern slope of Mauna Loa, the 13,680-foot volcano; and the snow-covered crater of Mauna Kea is in the background. In 1972 the picture was sold in aid of the World Wildlife Fund at a charity auction in Palm Beach, Florida. Its new owner, Mrs Enid Haupt, requested that it be rehung in the entrance hall of the Wildfowl Trust in honour of her brother, Mr Walter Annenberg, then US Ambassador to London. And there it still hangs.

In the 1950s I became involved in the work of the International Union for Conservation of Nature and Natural Resources. Its Survival Service Commission had been created by one of the founders of the Union itself, the great American conservationist, Harold Jefferson Coolidge, who has been a close colleague for the last 20 years. In 1962 I succeeded the indefatigable Colonel Leofric Boyle on his retirement as Chairman of the SSC.

Meanwhile international conservation suffered from a major handicap. It had no money. Max Nicholson, then head of the British governmental Nature Conservancy, and I travelled back from Switzerland together after one particularly fruitless meeting, in which the distinguished scientists who made up the IUCN Board (and who gave their valuable services to the Union free) had spent two and a half days at the Union's headquarters in Morges, on Lake Geneva, talking about how they could raise enough money to pay the secretaries till the end of the month. This was patently a great waste of their time and expertise. Max and I felt that a fully professional fund-raising organization was needed.

In America they have a saying that if two people come together and agree, they immediately form a society. If they disagree they form two societies. In this case we persuaded the world's leading conservationists to sign a solemn declaration called the Morges Manifesto, and soon thereafter we formed the World Wildlife Fund – an international fund-raising organization with National Appeals (now known as National Organizations) in a number of different countries (at present twenty-six). HRH The Prince of the Netherlands was the International President and HRH The Duke of Edinburgh was the President of the British National Appeal. I became Chairman of the Trustees of both, planned its structure and, among other things, drew its now quite well-known Panda symbol.

My biological training told me that an environmental crisis was on its way. It was becoming abundantly clear that all was not well with Planet Earth. It was not necessary to be an environmental expert to realize this. In the words of Ginger Rogers: 'You don't have to be a hen to recognize a bad egg.'

Then came Rachel Carson's *Silent Spring* and later a memorable meeting with her shortly before her death. I found myself thinking more ecologically and environmentally. The science of ecology had not been invented when I was learning biology; yet the instant its principles were enumerated I immediately realized the essential truth that all nature is interrelated, that we are a part of it, and need contact with it. Furthermore, because we are, as a species, the direct cause of so much of the environmental damage, we have a clear responsibility.

In my opinion this puts conservation, as a philosophical imperative – not merely as a device for saving our own skins – out in the mainstream of human progress. How much of it we can achieve, on the ground and in the oceans, is, of course, another story. As the American conservationist Aldo Leopold once wrote: 'Conservation is a state of harmony with a friend; you cannot cherish his right hand and chop off his left.'

The logo of the World Wildlife Fund, which I designed from a suggestion by Gerald Watterson, then the WWF's Secretary-General, in 1961.

Pintails on a hazy day. 1969. Oil on canvas. 20 × 30 in.

These were some that I saw on a misty winter's morning on the great marismas of the Coto Doñana in the delta of the River Guadalquivir in southern Spain, where great numbers of our northern ducks go in the winter. These vast marshlands have been under heavy pressure from drainage and development schemes which have involved conservationists – and in particular the World Wildlife Fund – in a continuing effort for the last twenty years. Keeping the marshes wet has been the perennial problem, as has the difficulty of allowing people to see what is being protected without prejudicing the protection.

Soon after the establishment of the World Wildlife Fund in 1961 I wrote a Conservation Creed which brought together some other reasons why we should spread the conservation message. It was as follows:

'*A voice crying in the wilderness?*

'What man did to the Dodo, and has since been doing to the Blue Whale and about 1,000 other kinds of animals, may or may not be morally wrong. But the conservation of nature is most important because of what nature does for man.

'I believe something goes wrong with man when he cuts himself off from the natural world. I think he knows it, and this is why he keeps gardens and window-boxes and house plants, and dogs and cats and budgerigars. Man does not live by bread alone. I believe he should take just as great pains to look after the natural treasures which inspire him as he does to preserve his man-made treasures in art galleries and museums. This is a responsibility we have to future generations, just as we are responsible for the safe-guarding of Westminster Abbey or the Mona Lisa.

'It has been argued that if the human population of the world continues to increase at its present rate, there will soon be no room for either wildlife or wild places, so why waste time, effort and money trying to conserve them now? But I believe that sooner or later man will learn to limit his own overpopulation. Then he will become much more widely concerned with optimum rather than maximum, quality rather than quantity, and will rediscover the need within himself for contact with wilderness and wild nature.

'No one can tell when this will happen. I am concerned that when it does, breeding stocks of wild animals and plants should still exist, preserved perhaps mainly in nature reserves and national parks, even in zoos and botanical gardens, from which to repopulate the natural environment man will then wish to re-create and rehabilitate.

'These are my reasons for believing passionately in the conservation of nature.

'All this calls for action of three kinds: more research in ecology, the setting aside of more land as effectively inviolate strongholds, and above all education. By calling attention to the plight of the world's wildlife, and by encouraging people to enrich their lives by the enjoyment of nature, it may be possible to accelerate both the change in outlook and the necessary action.

'It has been estimated that conservation all over the world needs each year £2 million. This is no astronomical figure. It is half the price of a V bomber, less than one twelfth the price of the new Cunarder, or the price of, say, three or four world-famous paintings.

'Much money is needed for relieving human suffering, but some is also needed for human fulfilment and inspiration. Conservation, like education and art, claims some proportion of the money we give to help others, including the as yet unborn.

'Even if I am wrong about the long-term prospects – if man were to fail to solve his own overpopulation problem, and reaches the stage 530 years hence when there will be standing room only on this earth – even then the conservation effort will have been worth while. It will have retained, at least for a time, some of the natural wonders. Measured in man-hours of enjoyment and inspiration this alone would be worth the effort. Many will have enjoyed the pictures even if the gallery is burnt down in the end.

'The community chest which seeks to make the gallery representative and maintains the fire-alarm system is the World Wildlife Fund.'

Not too much has changed since that was written in 1962; but public awareness everywhere is far greater than it used to be, in developing as well as in developed countries, and the long-term effects of conservation cannot be expected to become apparent immediately.

Plates 51 and 52 from the *Handbook of the Birds of Europe, the Middle East and North Africa.* 1976. Gouache on tinted paper. Each 12 × 8 in.

'Let the long contention cease, Geese are swans, and swans are geese.'

MATTHEW ARNOLD

Geese and swans are very different in appearance, even to a casual observer; yet in evolutionary terms they are quite close together. In their classic paper **The Family Anatidae** my friends Jean Delacour and Ernst Mayr divided the world's ducks, geese and swans into ten tribes, but placed the True Geese and the Swans in the same tribe – the **Anserini**. So technically Matthew Arnold was quite right. In terms of evolution a swan is closer to a goose than a Mallard is to a Tufted Duck, or than either of them is to a Goldeneye, for each of those is in a different tribe.

Left: *The Swans of the Western Palearctic.*

Cygnus olor Mute Swan:
1 Adult male
2 Adult female
3 First winter 4-9 months
4 Juvenile up to 4 months
5 Downy young
6 Adult ('Polish' morph.)
7 Juvenile ('Polish' morph.)
8 Downy young ('Polish' morph.)
Cygnus cygnus Whooper Swan:
9 Adult
10 Adult showing characteristic staining
11 2nd autumn
12 Juvenile at 7 months
13 Downy young
Cygnus columbianus bewickii Bewick's Swan:
14 Adult
15 Adult showing staining
16 2nd autumn
17 Juvenile at 7 months
18 Downy young

Right: *Five of the Grey Geese of the Western Palearctic.*

Anser fabalis Bean Goose:
A. f. fabalis Taiga Bean Goose
1 Adult
2 Adult showing extreme bill colouring and white frontal feathering
3 Juvenile up to 5-7 months
4 Downy young
A. f. rossicus Tundra Bean Goose
5 Adult
Anser brachyrhynchus Pink-footed Goose

6   Adult
7   Adult showing variation of bill pat-
     tern and white frontal feathering
8   Juvenile up to 5-7 months
8   Downy young
Anser anser Greylag Goose
A. a. anser Western Greylag Goose
10   Adult
11   Juvenile up to 5-7 months
12   Downy young
A. a. rubirostris Eastern Greylag Goose
13   Adult
14   Downy young

It is easy to be wise after the event; but
now that this plate has been reproduced, I
believe that I painted the pale edges to
the feathers of the back a little *too* pale,
particularly in the case of the Bean
Geese. And although individual Pinkfeet
vary considerably, I believe that many of
them are a little more blue-grey on the
back than I have made them.

The Second World Congress of the WWF was held in London in
1970. Its theme was 'All Life on Earth', and it was attended by a large
number of distinguished people. The presence of so many royal
personages gave the organization something of an élitist image, and it
was heavily attacked in an article claiming that too much of its money
went to administration. This was very damaging at the time but was
probably salubrious for the WWF, which has watched its overhead
expenses much more carefully ever since.

For me by far the most exciting feature of the Congress was to meet
Neil Armstrong, the first man to set foot on the Moon. My family and
I had sat up all night to watch him make his 'one small step for a man –
a giant leap for mankind'. Neil was a competition glider pilot and so
was I. I had won the British Gliding Championship in 1963 and was
runner-up in 1969. Later I was Chairman of the British Gliding
Association, and we sent Neil an invitation to attend our championship competitions and fly with us *hors concours*. He cabled back that
there was only one thing in the world he would rather do – and he was
doing it. A couple of months later we were watching him on our
television screen making that 'one small step'. And now, through the
WWF Congress, there was going to be a chance to meet him in person,

and delightfully unassuming we found him. This is part of what he told a rapt audience:

'To stand on the surface of the moon and look back at the earth high overhead is certainly an unusual and unique experience. Although it is very beautiful it is very remote and apparently very small. You might suspect that, in such a situation, the observer would dismiss the earth as relatively unimportant. Paradoxically the opposite conclusion has been reached by those individuals who have had the opportunity to share that view. We have all been struck by the simile of an oasis or an island; more importantly, it is the only island we know as a suitable home for man. The importance of protecting and saving that home has never been felt more strongly. Protection seems most required not

Left: *Thylacines*. Date unknown. Blue ink. About five-sevenths of size of drawing.

Below: *Puma*. 1968. Blue ink. About four-fifths of size of drawing.

Sketches for the endpapers of my autobiography *The Eye of the Wind* (Hodder and Stoughton, 1961). 1960. Black and blue ink. About three-quarters of size of drawing.

The animal species illustrated are: Peregrine Falcon, Pintail, Mallard, Jackson's Three-horned Chameleon, Bushbuck, Thecadactylus Gecko, Eyed Hawk Moth, Nene (or Hawaiian Goose), Housefly at risk from Chameleon.

from foreign aggressors or natural calamities, but rather from its own population . . .'

Much later I was in Washington DC for the launching of the Charles Lindbergh Foundation, established a short while after his death. Charles had been a great supporter of conservation. He was a trustee of WWF International and a member of my Survival Service Commission. Under the auspices of the IUCN, he had headed extremely effective conservation missions to a number of countries such as Madagascar, Chile and the Philippines. 'It works very well,' he once said, 'they think I am coming to talk about aviation and when I get there I talk about conservation.' He also attended several of the meetings of the International Whaling Commission, as the WWF representative.

The Foundation to be set up in his honour and memory was to be launched at a dinner in the huge Air and Space Museum of the Smithsonian Institution. The dinner was to be held on the second-

floor gallery looking out over the hanging aircraft, which included Lindbergh's famous 'Spirit of St Louis' and many of the space capsules. I was to pay tribute to Charles's outstanding work for conservation, and I thought it would be wise to visit the museum beforehand. That, they said, would present no problems. I should go to the museum and ask for the Director – a Mr Michael Collins – who would be happy to show me the layout. Mr Collins was extremely and meticulously helpful, and I left him without realizing that he was the Mike Collins who had been orbiting the moon while Neil Armstrong and Buzz Aldrin were making their kangaroo hops down on its surface. When I met him again at the dinner I owned up to not having realized, and he said, 'it's sometimes easier when you don't get recognized'.

As the WWF became better known, it became necessary for me to give lectures and make speeches and chair meetings, all of which interfered with my time for painting. By dint of much delegation, I

Hispaniolan Solenodon. Date unknown. Blue ink. About three-quarters of size of drawing.

Opposite: *The natural world of man.* 1963. Oil on canvas. 15½ × 28 in.

The picture represents man's dilemma in his relationship with nature. The problem is seen as triangular. At the pointed end are ethical responsibilities to save the animals facing extinction – the Blue Whale, the Whooping Crane, Hispaniolan Solenodon, Tuatara, Galapagos Tortoise, Rhinoceros. From there the scope broadens to encompass communities of animals – wild geese, fishes, antelopes – and their relationship to flowers and trees and to water and soil. All are a part of the biosphere in which man must live. The water is in the cumulus cloud (under which a white glider soars), and the river system with its tree-like formation, bearing leaves, and its foam-polluted tributary, is echoed by the pattern of soil erosion caused by the over-grazing of cattle being herded below with their accompanying dust. There are suggestions of urbanization and industrialization (including an electric bulb, a television screen and control knob). A ship gives out oil pollution, a plane is spraying toxic chemicals, and there is a rocket missile. The peak of Everest ('because it is there') peeps from behind the mushroom cloud whose fall-out is destroying the people spreading from the population explosion beyond the broad end of the triangle. 'The pill' is there too.

The three-dimensional triangle itself is carried by arms in a sea of space dominated by the moon, with a nearby sputnik. There is a space traveller's horizon to the earth, and in the right-hand corner a new galaxy is born. Man, with one white hand and one black, stands transfixed before this vast and terrifying pyramid of problems.

Right: *Red-breasted Geese.* 1976. Watercolour in diary. Page 8 × 6 in.

I have always been able to draw and listen intently at the same time. So I like to take drawing tools, either for line drawing, or for watercolour, to meetings. The only time when I cannot use them is when I am in the chair, for one must then be looking to see who wants to speak next. But if someone else is chairman, it is nice to come out of the meeting with 'something to show for it'. This little drawing of six adult Red-breasted Geese and one immature was made in my diary during a conference of the International Waterfowl Research Bureau in Alushta in the Crimea in the autumn of 1976.

could manage to get the administrative work done by others. I had learned two important maxims and used them whenever possible among the many brilliant people who were prepared to give some of their time to a cause they believed in. The first is: 'If you want work well done, select a busy man. The other kind has no time'; the second: 'If you want work well done, give it to an individual, never to a committee.' In this democratic world the second maxim is harder to stick to. I had long ago learned that no one in life is perfect, but one must be thankful if they do well what you want them to do; and if they do they must be praised, because almost everyone does their best work when they think they are doing well.

The kinds of speeches and lectures I am expected to make have to cover the whole range of environmental conservation, from human overpopulation to endangered species. They should be full of facts and figures, but I find that audiences do not easily assimilate facts and figures (especially figures). They seem more likely to stay listening if they think there will be a chance to laugh from time to time. The trouble is that I do not remember jokes, and this gave rise to a little notebook labelled 'Funnies and Quotes'. It had its prototype in my schooldays when my form master at Oundle – a charming gentle

Branta ruficollis
Krasnozobaya Kazarka

Peter Scott.

creature called Sammy Squire – encouraged all his boys to keep a 'Tag Book' in which we wrote, often in Latin, 'wise saws and modern instances'. Alas, I cannot find my Tag Book, but its newly established counterpart now has 450 entries which range from '"Who was that lady I saw you with last night?" "That was no night. It was a total eclipse of the sun"', to 'I shot an arrow into the air – and missed.' It includes the story which Frank Muir told at a Wildfowl Trust Dinner – the Pig Story, which I stole and confabulated as a personal experience, to illustrate the difficulties of communication. I was driving, I say, along a narrow lane in Gloucestershire when I came to another car coming the opposite way. There was barely room for the two to pass so I pulled in to my side of the road (it is no good saying 'to the left' if you tell the story, say, in the United States) and stopped. As the other car inched past, its driver – it was a lady driver – wound down her window and shouted 'Pig!' I was taken aback by this, as I did not think I deserved any such comment. However, I drove on, thinking all sorts of unkind things about lady drivers in general and that one in particular. Round the next corner, I ran slap into a pig.

When I came to talk about the environmental problems which beset us – human overpopulation ('whatever your cause, it's a lost cause unless we can stabilize the human population'), pollution ('the profit of doom' and 'the effluent society'), poverty ('the ever-widening poverty gap'), it seemed necessary to find a lighter side whenever possible, although none of them is a laughing matter. I found myself recounting the agonized cry of the industrialist, 'you know, this pollution business is costing us the EARTH', and Mark Twain's 'first get your facts right, then you can distort them as you choose.'

In the World Wildlife Fund there were two points of view. Many of our Trustees felt that the organization was created for saving wild animals from extinction, and arguably this could not be done without saving their habitats as well. These were the main objectives and to get more deeply involved in environmental problems such as 'POP, POL

Below left: *White-tailed Gnu*. Date unknown. Black ball-point. Actual size of drawing.

Below: *Quagga*. Date unknown. Blue ink. About two-thirds of size of drawing.

Below right: *Przewalski's Horses*. Date unknown. Blue ink. Actual size of drawing.

Brent Geese at Foulness. 1969. Oil on canvas. 20 × 30 in.

The first assembly point in autumn of the dark-bellied race of the Brent Goose is usually at Foulness on the Essex coast, an area which came under pressure in 1969 and in 1979 as one of the potential sites for London's Third Airport. The Brents, which breed in the Arctic, were greatly depleted in numbers, in part perhaps because of a catastrophic decrease in their *Zostera* seaweed winter food, but also because of hunting. In 1957 the population of this race was estimated at about 10,000. However, they have taken to feeding on grass and winter wheat fields, and by the winter of 1979-80, with the help of protection, the population had increased to around 200,000.

and POV' could only lead us into divisive arguments which were irrelevant to the WWF. The other school of thought believed that fighting conservation issues without tackling the basic causes of the crisis was liable to be a waste of time.

Some of the National Organizations of the WWF took one line, others the opposite; a few became involved in the nuclear energy argument, others with the more extreme campaigns mounted by the humane societies. It seemed that WWF policy should be briefly restated. I was asked to do this, and suggested that it could be done in 200 words. The following statement was finally adopted:

The concern of the World Wildlife Fund is the natural environment – its animals and plants and the ecological web which binds them together with climate, soil and water into those healthy ecosystems which for centuries Mankind has characterized by the word 'Nature'.

WWF pays particular attention to endangered species and those which have been seriously depleted by the impact of Man, and to endangered natural habitats.

At the same time WWF is acutely aware of the causal factors which make nature conservation so necessary and urgent – the problems of human population increase, of high technology agriculture, of industrialization and urbanization, of pollution, of misuse and waste of resources and energy, of famine and of poverty.

If solutions to these problems can be found, WWF's aims will be more easily achieved, for it is clear that the conservation of nature cannot be dealt with in isolation from the human condition.

But in view of the limited funds at present available, WWF's priority projects are mainly, though not exclusively, directed towards wildlife – defined as animals and plants and their wild habitats – and towards the promotion of public awareness of the immediate dangers that threaten nature and the steps necessary to avert them.

To the pattern of World Wildlife Fund, International Union for Conservation of Nature, and Wildfowl Trust, I must add another body with which I have been connected for a number of years. It is the Fauna Preservation Society, based in London, which with a comparatively small budget seems to me to achieve a great deal of practical

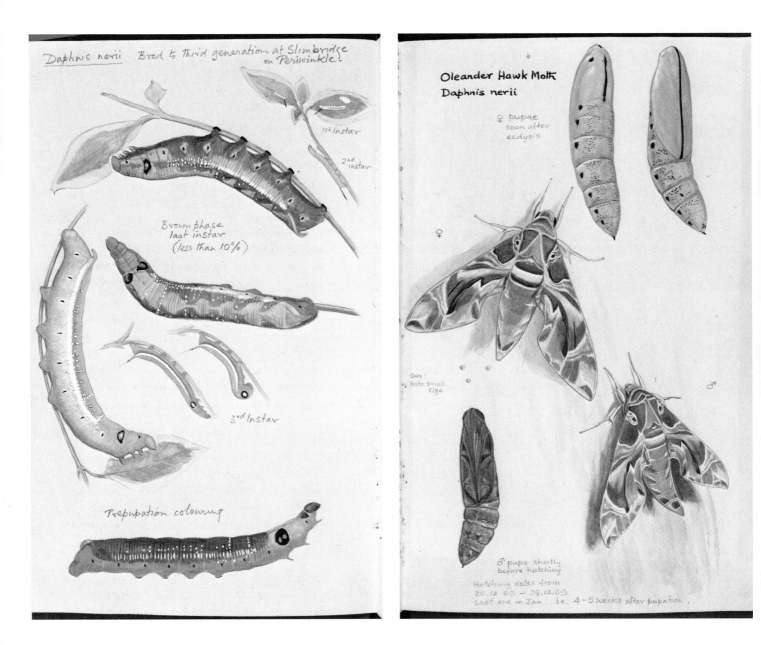

Daphnis nerii Bred to third generation at Slimbridge on Periwinkle!

1st instar

2nd instar

Brown phase last instar (less than 10%)

3rd Instar

Prepupation colouring

Oleander Hawk Moth
Daphnis nerii

♀ pupae soon after ecdysis

♀

Ova: Note small size

♂ pupa shortly before hatching

Hatching dates from 20.12.69 – 28.12.69. Last one in Jan. i.e. 4–5 weeks after pupation.

♂

conservation. Its Secretary, my friend of more than 30 years, is Richard Fitter (who also spans the WWF and IUCN), and its publication *Oryx*, edited by his tireless wife Maisie, is one of the best journals in the whole field of conservation. The Arabian Oryx is their symbol, and in conjunction with the WWF, the FPS mounted Operation Oryx to take into captivity the last few wild Arabian Oryx. Fortunately these antelope breed easily in captivity, and the zoos in Phoenix, San Diego and Los Angeles have been able to start the last phase of the operation by sending some of the animals back to special reserves in the Middle East.

I was invited to become Chairman of the Council of the FPS, mainly, I think, to maintain a visible unity of purpose between these various organizations, and FPS Council Meetings have been among the most dynamic conservation meetings I regularly attend. This is

Oleander Hawk Moths: left, larvae; right, pupae and imagos. 1969. Watercolour in diary. Each page 8 × 6 in.

Since my school days I have had a great interest in hawk moths. One of the rarest in Britain is the Oleander Hawk Moth, which from time to time reaches Britain from its strongholds in Asia and Africa. From the pictures in books I had always admired the species; but I had never seen it alive. In 1969, during a visit to Qatar to look at a captive herd of Arabian Oryx, I was taken to the summer palace of Sheikh Qasem bin Hamad al Thani. In the garden were a number of oleander bushes, and, in company with Richard Fitter, I walked up to the first.

'You know, we ought to look for the larvae of the Oleander Hawk Moth,' I said. And there, right in front of me, was a fully fed larva as thick as my finger. After a careful search, I managed to find 12 caterpillars. These were probably all the offspring of one female moth. Most of them pupated before we left Qatar two days later, though I remember that when we flew on to India I had to stop to collect fresh oleander leaves outside the airport at New Delhi for the last two or three of the larvae. About twelve days later the first of the pupae hatched, and from then on for the whole of the following summer we were able to breed Oleander Hawk Moths at home. The food plant we used was a variegated periwinkle.

During a short spell in hospital for a minor operation, I was able to study them closely, and to make these drawings in my diary. At the end of the third generation it was impossible to obtain a successful pairing; but I had been able to supply many of my lepidopterist friends with eggs which they successfully reared to maturity.

perhaps because we spend more time discussing field projects than administration and finance.

To maintain the link the other way, Richard Fitter has been the Convenor of the Steering Committee of the Survival Service Commission. This commission of the IUCN has as its straightforward aim, 'the prevention of the extinction of species, sub-species and discrete populations, thereby maintaining genetic diversity'. In pursuit of this aim we began to list the species in danger in a series of loose-leaf books called the Red Data Books. We produced a volume for Mammals, another for Birds, one for Reptiles and Amphibia, and one for Fish – so that all the vertebrate animals have been covered. Now we are embarking on invertebrates and on plants. The degree of threat has been colour coded – the most endangered on red sheets, those rare but not in immediate danger on white sheets, those still numerous but greatly depleted on yellow sheets (amber for caution), those about which we know too little on grey sheets (grey areas), and those formerly in danger but now out of danger on green sheets. It could be said that the object of the exercise is to get all the animals in the Red Data Books onto green sheets. Then we could wind up the whole operation.

But we recognize that merely listing those in danger is only stage one. We then have to find out why they are threatened and finally persuade the relevant authorities to carry out the necessary measures to prevent their disappearance. To discover what needs to be done we have a programme entitled Necessary Elements to Eliminate the Decline of Species (NEEDS), and for the final stage we have a programme for Action to Prevent eXtinction (APX). The members of our 4 Specialist Groups – more than a thousand of them – are helping us to get these programmes under way.

We are frequently told that the emphasis in conservation should not be on endangered species but rather on ecosystems, which if saved will save many endangered species at the same time. We recognize the truth of this, but the fact is that people understand what is meant by extinction and are easily motivated to prevent it, whether they are decision-makers or supporters of an appeal for funds. When Guy Mountfort had the idea of mounting a campaign to save the last remaining tigers it was immensely successful. The WWF raised more than £1 million and the Indian Government supported it to the tune of several millions more. The method used was to set aside a substantial number of special reserves, which served not only to save the tigers that lived there but the whole pyramid of plants and animals on top of which the tiger stood as the principal predator.

When the WWF launched a campaign a few years later to save the tropical rain forests of the world – which are being cut down at the rate of 50 acres a minute day and night – it had considerably less impact because people could not visualize them as they could a tiger.

It will be many years before any real assessment of the success of all these bodies with their acronyms and their projects can be made. We do not yet know whether they are going the right way about it. Sometimes we doubt if they are, but it is perhaps worth pointing out

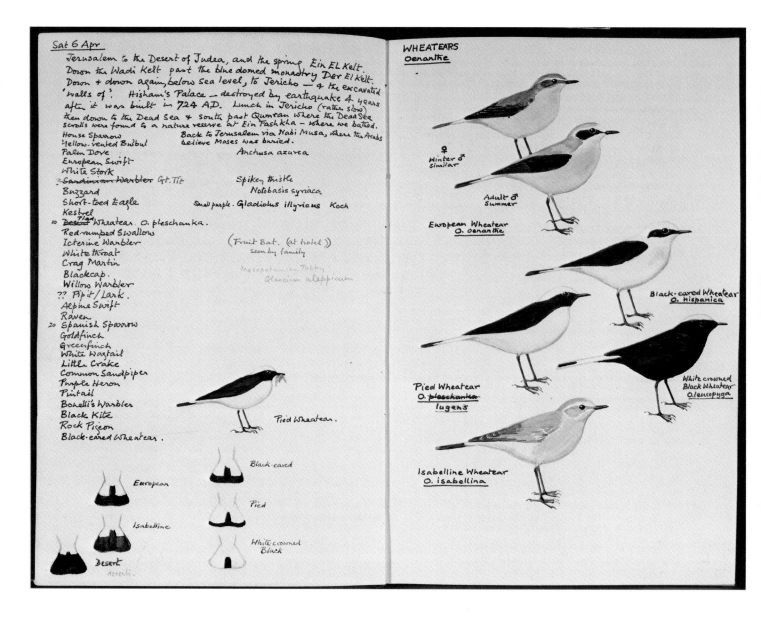

Wheatears. 1968. Watercolour in Diary. Page 8 × 6 in.

that it is often possible to achieve a specific end successfully by quite different means.

The story is told that four students of Birmingham University were each given a pocket barometer and told to ascertain the height of the red brick clock-tower. They were a student of physics, a student of engineering, a student of mathematics and a student of the Faculty of Arts. The student of physics read the barometer at the bottom, then climbed to the top, read it again and calculated the height. The student of engineering acquired a ball of string, climbed to the top, lowered the barometer on the string, and then measured the string. The student of maths dropped the barometer from the top and timed its fall with a stop-watch, from which he calculated the height. The student of the Faculty of Arts went to find the Caretaker and said, 'I say, old boy, how high's the tower?' and then gave him the barometer as a present. They all got the answer right.

During a visit to Israel in 1968, I saw a number of different wheatear species. I try to list the species seen each day, and in this case made myself a quick field-guide to the wheatear tail patterns to help identification as we motored round the country. On the opposite side I painted the wheatear species that we actually *did* see on the trip.

Yellow Wagtails in Saudi Arabia. 1974.
Watercolour in diary. Page 8 × 6 in.

During a run of visits to Saudi Arabia in the mid-1970s to arouse interest and support for conservation, I was privileged to stay at the British Embassy in Jeddah with Alan and Anne Rothnie. At the end of April 1974, there were numbers of Yellow Wagtails apparently of several different races to be seen together on the lawn. My diagnosis of the Spanish Yellow Wagtail, *Motacilla flava iberiae*, was probably incorrect, as Saudi Arabia is far off its range; the bird was probably a Blue-headed Wagtail, *Motacilla flava flava*. I'm afraid that I have given several of the birds too long a tail; but I am always carried away by their slender elegance.

In the autumn of 1979 a conference was held in San Diego, the third in a series on breeding endangered species in captivity. It addressed itself to two themes: how to establish self-sustaining populations in captive conditions without having to draw on wild stocks, and how to reintroduce captive-bred animals into the wild. The second one postulates a 'wild' to put them in. We established first of all that it was infinitely worth keeping viable populations going even if there was no prospect of releasing them into a wild situation. Tigers in zoos only was clearly preferable to no tigers left alive anywhere. Those who believe that endangered species should not be kept in zoos because it would never be possible to let them out again were ignoring an important factor – time. When the 11th Duke of Bedford collected all the Père David's Deer in captivity – 16 animals – from the world's zoos, there were none left alive in China, and no habitat was available for them. He could not then have known that 70 years later the Government of the People's Republic of China would be considering

M.f. feldegg. Black-headed. (Largest)
M.f. flavissima. Yellow
M.f. pygmea. Egyptian
    (or cinereocapilla Ashy-headed)
M.f. flava. Blue-headed.
M.f. lutea Kirghiz steppe.

♀

M.f. thunbergi
   Grey-headed
M.f. iberiae
   Spanish (or flava Blue-headed)

Races of the Yellow Wagtail. Motacilla flava, all seen together at one time in the garden of the British Embassy at Jeddah.
27th April 1975

re-creating a reserve for them. He merely thought it wrong to let them die out, so he built up a herd of several hundred in Woburn Park, from which many zoos have received breeding nuclei, including the Peking Zoo.

The tremendous advances in captive-breeding techniques since the earlier conferences (in Jersey and London) were one of the surprises at San Diego. The familiar arguments were trotted out by conservationists who do not believe that species extinction can be averted in this way; but time and again examples of successful breeding were reported from species that had never been known to breed in captivity before, or had only bred sparingly in a few places. These included many primate species, many cats, with some notable successes in breeding large numbers of Cheetahs, and such difficult creatures as duikers and insectivores, as well as falcons, cranes and flamingos. They say that familiarity breeds contempt, but it was Noel Coward who pointed out that without a *little* familiarity you can't breed anything.

White Rhinoceros. Date unknown. Black ball-point. About four-fifths of size of drawing.

Père David's Deer. Date unknown. Black ink. About three-fifths of size of drawing.

Nenes in the sun on the slopes of Mauna Loa.
1968. Oil on board. 20 × 30 in.

It seems that the Wildfowl Trust has played a significant part in preventing the extinction of the Hawaiian Goose (or Nene), partly by drawing attention to the importance of protection measures in Hawaii, and partly by breeding the species successfully in England. From three original birds and four extra males later, about 1,300 have been bred in captivity and 200 sent to repopulate the Hawaiian island of Maui.

Cheetah. 1976. Black ink. About four-fifths of size of drawing.

Peter Scott, 1970

Chapter 4   Travels and Encounters

'*Vectatio, iterque et mutata regio vigorem dant.*'
(Voyaging, travel and change of place impart vigour.)

SENECA

Philippa and I have been wonderfully fortunate in being able to travel so widely. This has been due in part to making television films of wildlife, in part to my voluntary work for conservation, and in part to Lars-Eric Lindblad and his beautiful ship, the *Lindblad Explorer*. I have been invited to go as naturalist and lecturer, and Phil has also been on the staff when we go, helping to keep the 90 passengers happy during their cruise. We have made 19 trips lasting from two to five weeks each, and we have become very fond of 'the little red ship'. At 2,500 tons she is not so little, but as cruise ships go, she is a mini-liner. For ten years she has been taking her passengers to places where passenger ships do not normally go, like the Arctic and the Antarctic, and the more remote Pacific Islands. She also goes 2,000 miles up the Amazon, and has, sadly, twice run aground in the largely uncharted waters of Antarctica.

We have been in her to the Arctic, once circumnavigating Spitsbergen and finding Barnacle and Pink-footed Geese there, and SCUBA diving off the north coast. On that expedition I dived at Bear Island, and at Scoresbysund in north Greenland, where Rod Salm and I swam through a cave under an iceberg. The blues and greens were marvellously beautiful, and little brown shrimps were spaced out evenly all through the ice tunnel, stationary, like hoverflies. We had another dive under great lily pads of pancake ice at Angmagssalik in south-east Greenland.

Wonderful though Greenland's icy mountains, the glaciers, the musk oxen and the migrating Pinkfeet were, the underwater scenes stand out most in my memory. Some years after that we were in the Arctic again – in Alaska with the *Explorer*. The profusion and diversity of sea birds was superb, but again SCUBA diving with Steller's Sea Lions, and later with Pribilof Fur Seals among the forests of kelp, were the most unforgettable adventures.

With Lindblad Travel we have made four expeditions to the Antarctic – three of them in the *Explorer*. On one of these I was able to take Philippa and our daughter Dafila into my father's huts at Cape Evans

Red-breasted Geese in the big field below the quarry at Sinoie. 1970. Oil on board. 18 × 14 in.

Who knows what the scene looks like to the avian eye, but this may be what another Redbreast, flying in to land with the massed flock of its own kind and of Whitefronts, could see on the afternoon of Friday 12 December 1969 in Romania. It was also a view I could get through a telescope from further up the slope on the first day that I had ever seen Redbreasted Geese in thousands. It was a day I shared with my Dutch fellow goose enthusiast Tom Lebret, and it led to further visits in the winters of 1971, 1973 and 1977.

'The stickers all say "We've been to Slimbridge".' 1978. Black ink. About three-quarters of size of drawing.

and Hut Point (where the new settlement of 'McMurdo City' has been established). All the historic huts round McMurdo Sound in the Ross Sea have been looked after most beautifully by the New Zealanders from Scott Base. To go into them, especially the one at Cape Evans, was, we found, very moving. Phil and I went into it again in January 1979 – it was my third visit and once again I felt a strange uplifting of spirit. With all the polar hardships and tragedies, I felt a happy aura in the place. There had been jollity and fun there, as well as anxiety and foreboding. It is as if it had been occupied only a few weeks ago, for the cold preserves everything very well.

Once again my Antarctic memories are dominated by SCUBA diving there. In 1978 we had two dives, one to watch Gentoo Penguins flying past underwater, and the other to watch Adélie Penguins, which did not dare approach us, evidently equating us with Leopard Seals, whereas on land they are delightfully tame.

The *Explorer* is in the Arctic during the northern summer and in the Antarctic in the southern summer. In between she must cross the Equator and has a chance to explore the Pacific Islands with their fascinating people and their incredible coral reefs. For us snorkelling and diving on these reefs is one of life's major delights, with the ship as a base and using its rubber zodiacs to swim from. In the last ten years we have visited a large proportion of the archipelagos in the Pacific and Indian Oceans and sampled their amazing diversity of reef fishes, which in some ways are so bird-like.

Right: *Butterfly fish and an Angel Fish.* 1980.
Blue ink. 8 × 5 in.

Below: *Adélie Penguin.* 1968. Blue ink. About
three-quarters of size of drawing.

Adelie Penguin.
Ecstatic Display. Torgeson Island.   February 1968

Phil and I first went snorkelling together 24 years ago. Our first look
into the underwater world was on the Great Barrier Reef off Cairns.
Since then we have become moderately knowledgeable about coral
reef fishes. Our speciality has been Butterfly fish, Angel fish, Cherub
fish and Clown fish. In particular we have used the Butterfly fish as a
comparative measure of the diversity of reefs. Many different Butterfly fish species may be found swimming in pairs on the same reef. It
seems that their food requirements are slightly different; thus we
count up the species as a rough measure of reef richness. Fifteen
species is high. We found 17 on one short swim in Tonga, and have
recently marked up the same at Heron Island on the Great Barrier over
a week.

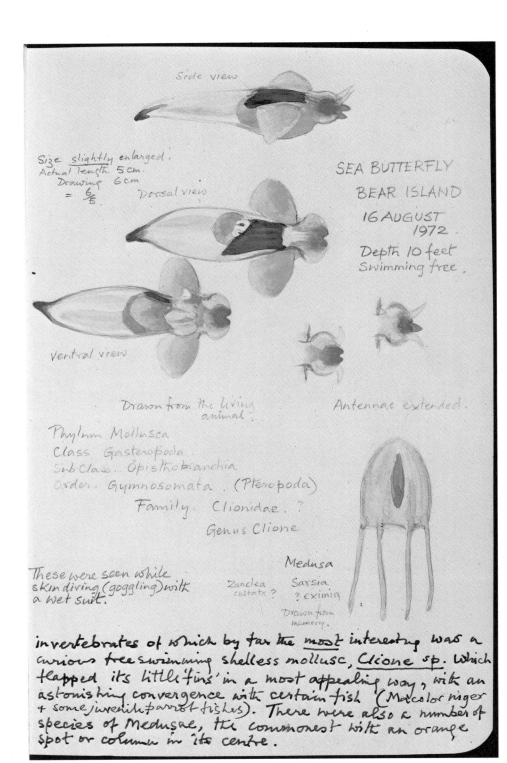

Side view

Size slightly enlarged.
Actual length 5 cm.
Drawing 6 cm
= 6/5

Dorsal view

SEA BUTTERFLY

BEAR ISLAND

16 AUGUST
1972.

Depth 10 feet
Swimming free.

Ventral view

Drawn from the living
animal.

Antennae extended.

Phylum Mollusca
Class Gasteropoda.
Sub Class. Opisthobranchia
Order. Gymnosomata. (Pteropoda)
Family. Clionidae. ?
Genus Clione

Medusa

Zanclea   Sarsia
costata ?   ? eximia

These were seen while
skin diving (goggling) with
a wet suit.

Drawn from
memory.

invertebrates of which by far the most interesting was a
curious free swimming shelless mollusc, Clione sp. which
flapped its 'little fins' in a most appealing way, with an
astonishing convergence with certain fish (Melcolor niger
+ some juvenile parrot fishes). There were also a number of
species of Medusae, the commonest with an orange
spot or column in its centre.

Sea Butterfly or Pteropod (Clione) at Bear Island. 1972. Watercolour in diary. Page 8 × 6 in.

During an Arctic cruise in the **Lindblad Explorer**, on which I was travelling, with Philippa, as naturalist and lecturer, Rod Salm and I put on wet suits and dived in Spitsbergen, Greenland and Bear Island. In one of the two Greenland dives we swam through a cave in a stranded iceberg at Scoresbysund. At Bear Island we only had time for snorkelling.

The details of this delightful free-swimming waterbaby we found are told on the page of my diary.

In July and August 1976, Philippa and I made a wonderful voyage in the **Lindblad Explorer**. It began at Prince Rupert in British Columbia, went up the coast of Alaska into the Bering Sea, across the Arctic Circle, and up to the Arctic ice, then down through the Aleutian Islands to Japan. From there we went south to the Bonin Islands, the Marianas, the Carolines and the Indonesian Islands, and across to Bali whence we flew home.

I was able to dive off the Alaskan Coast with Steller's Sea Lions, and with the Fur Seals on the Pribilof Islands. Further south we had fantastic diving and snorkelling on the coral reefs. My diary for 21 August 1976, when we were at Helen Reef, reads, 'One of the finest reef drop-offs on which I ever swam . . . I had about an hour snorkelling followed by three-quarters of an hour SCUBA diving to 60 feet down the vertical cliff with Soames, with Phil and Nancy up above us. Then more snorkelling. It was a morning to remember.'

The Blue Jewel Fish (**M. tuka**) were in big shoals. To appreciate the colour of these wonderful little fish one must dive down to about ten feet so as to be at their level and close enough. The scarlet dorsal fin of **M. dispar** viewed at a distance can appear quite black. The pointed snouts of the males can be folded back and the mouth opened to disclose its white interior, but for what function I do not know.

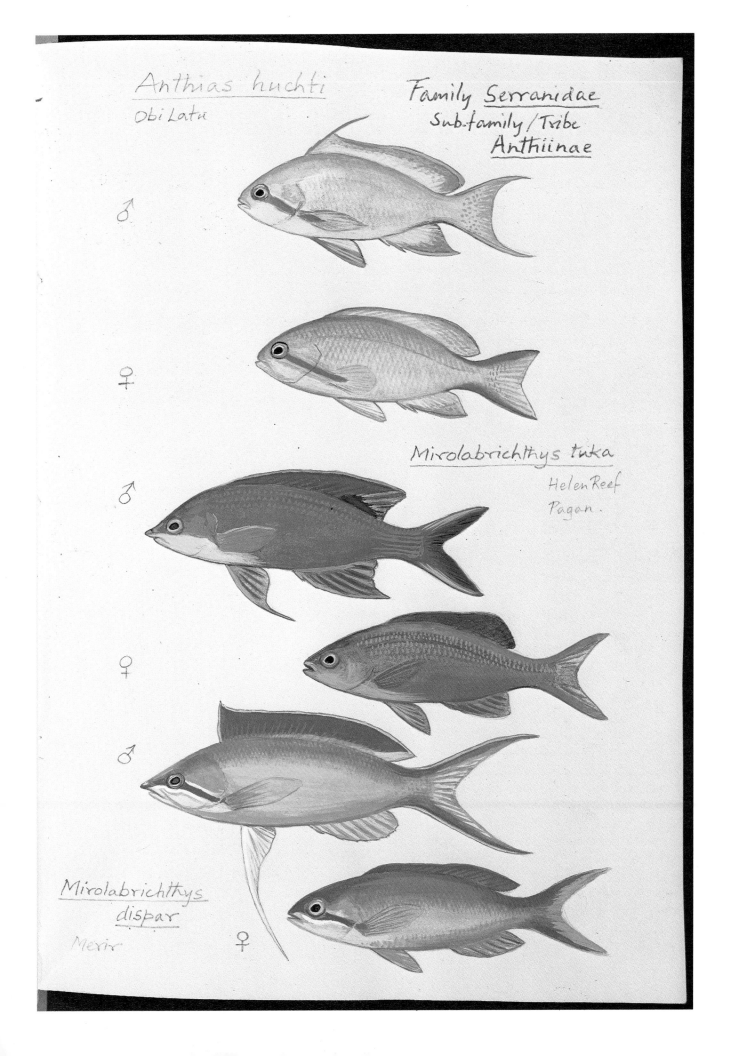

Anthias huchti
Obi Latu

Family Serranidae
Sub-family / Tribe
Anthiinae

♂

♀

Mirolabrichthys tuka
Helen Reef
Pagan.

♂

♀

♂

Mirolabrichthys
dispar
Merir

♀

It is strange that the fish that interest most people are sharks. They are, of course, very graceful creatures; but the appeal seems primarily to be because they occasionally eat people. We have our fair share of shark stories, but have not yet been eaten by one. One night in the Bahamas when my daughter and I were swimming arm in arm with a torch, a Lemon Shark came at top speed towards the torch, and turned away at the last moment. So close was it that when I instantly switched off the torch that had clearly attracted it, Dafila asked if my hand was all right, as she thought the shark might have taken it and the torch.

Sharks are unpredictable, people say, which is another way of saying we do not know enough about them yet to predict what they will do. My technique is to keep facing them and whenever possible to appear to show aggression by making towards them. On the day I meet a hungry Great White Shark I know my technique is unlikely to be successful. But by and large sharks are, I believe, a good deal less dangerous than London traffic. I once heard an expert diver telling a novice that the only way to deal with a shark was to look him straight in the eye and 'show him you are not afraid of him'. 'Oh,' said the newcomer, 'I couldn't be that deceitful.'

During our trip to Antarctica in the *Lindblad Explorer* at the beginning of 1979, when skirting the continent on our way from South America, via the Antarctic Peninsula and the Ross Sea, to New Zealand, we happened upon two whaling factory ships, one from Japan and the other from New Zealand. An hour or so later we sighted a whale-catcher, which turned out to be Russian and was in the act of stalking a pod of Minke Whales, the smallest of the baleen whales, which do not grow much longer than 25 feet.

As we were approaching, we saw the harpoon fired and one of the whales hit. For four and a half minutes it surfaced occasionally, spouting blood, then it sounded, diving deep. Eight minutes after being struck it was hauled up to the surface tail first and seemed to be dead. The whale-catcher already had two dead Minke Whales lying alongside. By this time we were within a hundred yards. Every camera on our ship had recorded the scene. Every passenger had seen the death of a whale at first hand. It was something I had never seen before. Thinking of all those speeches I had made on behalf of the WWF to the International Whaling Commission down the years, telling them what damage they had done to the populations of the great whales, I now realized how much their impact had suffered because I had never seen the real thing.

On the way back from that Antarctic expedition, Phil and I broke our journey in Hawaii to accept an invitation to swim with Humpback Whales. The arrangements had been made by Dr Sylvia Earle, marine botanist and one of the world's most distinguished and experienced divers. We were to be the guests of Jim Luckey of the Lahaina Restoration Foundation at the Pioneer Inn in Lahaina, on the island of Maui – where, on the Haleakala Crater, our Slimbridge-bred Hawaiian Geese had been released.

Diary entries for 25 February 1979. Watercolour. Page 8 × 6 in.

Sun 25ᵗʰ Feb.   **The Dolphin Day — with Whale Songs.**

were to have gone with the Imax team again, but Sylvia (who planned
whole adventure for us at the Ashkabad conference) thought we
ought to hear Whales singing - which of course we had not done
the previous day   So she arranged for us to go out with Peter
Tyack (one of Roger Payne's team) and Bernie Krause (who makes
whale recordings and is an electronic composer) in their small
Zodiak, with Sylvia herself and her little daughter Mouse. At
10 we left from alongside the Carthaginian moored near the
Lahaina Pierhead & the Pioneer Inn.
The centre of the Zodiak was occupied by a huge box containing
recording gear & radio equipment. This was the Zodiak which
Jim & Al Giddings had used when making Gentle Giants of the
Pacific.
We started by listening and at once heard a Whale singing
& a second more distant one in the background. Later
simultaneous songs could be heard.   Peter told us that
songs are constantly changing but that there is virtually no
difference between the songs of individual whales. Song records
are dated to within a week, but so far it has not been possible to
distinguish one singer from another.
John had been directing the various boats + plotting whale movements
every day from a hill SE of Lahaina and we had frequently been in
touch with him from the SportDiver.
In the course of the morning we had tried to approach several
turtles but had seen nothing larger than a Tiny cryptic
pretending to be a piece of seaweed and anxious to use as
cover. I must say he looked to be very vulnerable once
we detected that he was a free-swimming animal.
During this swim we also saw a Venus's Girdle
(Ctenophora) which was superbly curled when I first found it,
& a much smaller Sea Gooseberry.
Later we had some dolphins near us and I hung from
a rope on the side of the Zodiac. At first I saw nothing &
found the whole exercise pretty exhausting. However we
were eventually close enough & I had a rather short view
of a pair of Dolphins at about 30 ft range. Their most
notable feature was that they had white tips to a fairly short
snout. Furthermore the white areas were lowest under the dorsal
and rose towards head + tail. Peter Tyack thought they

Overleaf: *Self-portrait with Humpbacks.* 1979.
Oil on canvas. 28 × 36 in.

In March 1979, after a long Antarctic cruise in the *Lindblad Explorer*, we broke the journey back home in the Hawaiian Islands in order to swim with the Humpback Whales off Maui.

In the course of one twenty-minute period of snorkelling, seven whales came to look at us. On this occasion there were three. At the surface in the centre I am swimming parallel with them, while at the left Philippa is taking photographs of them. All three were well-grown whales, though the deepest of the three seemed the largest, and the one above it might have been a well-grown calf.

Humpbacks grow to more than 40 feet long, and can weigh up to 45 tons. Throughout our meetings with them they were always absolutely gentle, and at no time did they give us any cause to be afraid. For both of us it was a totally unforgettable experience. Overleaf ⟶

The waters off Lahaina are well known as a mating and calving ground for Humpback Whales, and the town has a history dating from the heyday of whaling, when the over-exploitation was at its height. At present Lahaina is enjoying a boom based on the new interest in living whales, which have become a kind of symbol of survival. 'If we can't save the great whales, what hope is there of saving the human species?' so the argument goes.

We were to go out in a boat chartered by a team of film-makers, and Phil and I were asked when in the water to 'keep out of the shot, because you are not in the script'. Here is part of the entry from my diary:

'More whales were in sight some distance away. There were three groups and some dolphins. One group was flipper-splashing. The groups seemed to be meeting and we stopped in the middle. The camera was launched, then Phil and I went into the water together. We held hands to keep in quick communication. The people on board were yelling, which is thought to attract whales, and pointing. We turned that way, and deep down we saw, almost simultaneously, two dim white lines. These were the leading edges of the pectorals of one of a pair of Humpbacks. The closest they came was perhaps thirty feet and they looked superb, moving very slowly and gently. At no time did we feel the least bit apprehensive. It was intensely exciting just to be with these fifty-foot creatures. They passed us by and very quickly disappeared with lazy tail flaps.

'As soon as they had gone, we saw the people on the boat pointing again, and almost at once another pair came in sight. Phil broke off to photograph them with her Nikonos. I swam closer as they came directly towards us. I thought, maybe, I was a little *too* directly ahead of them, and turned to the right, thereby passing immediately ahead of Phil, who was taking downward pictures. Then I turned back towards them and the whales crossed slowly ahead of us, rolling slightly away from us to take a good look. I gazed into the eye of the nearer, smaller whale – it may have been twenty feet away and the end of its pectoral fin was a good deal closer. As they passed ahead of Phil I saw the eye move from me to her and a crescent of white showed just behind the brown iris. That the animal was close enough to see the white of its eye immediately struck me.' Altogether, we saw at least five whales, and possibly seven, in a twenty-minute swim.

A few weeks later, on the eve of the International Whaling Commission meeting in London, I was allowed to address a rally of 12,000 people in Trafalgar Square about the stand we had to take at the meetings. I summed up what I felt in the following personal statement about whales:

'What we have done to the great whales in the sacred name of commerce is an affront to human dignity, a debasement of human values and sensibility. These magnificent animals – almost certainly the largest that have ever existed on earth, and now recognized as the

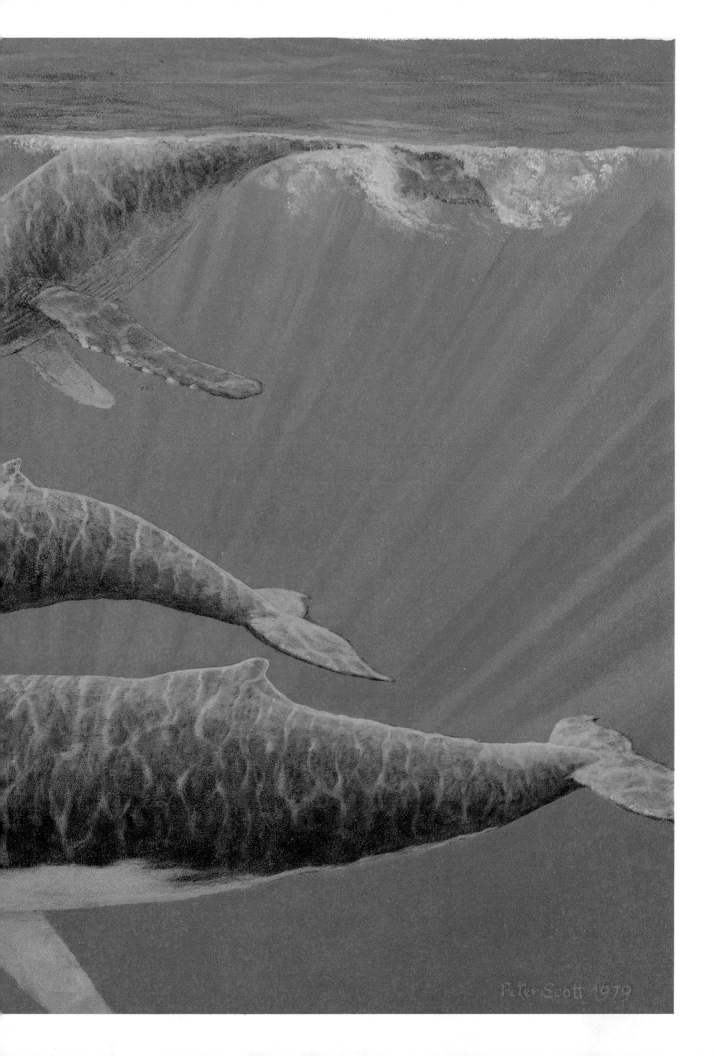

Peter Scott 1979

possessors of outstanding intelligence – have been brought to the brink of extinction by killing methods of appalling cruelty, through the greed of mankind. I have personally witnessed and timed the death throes of a Minke Whale – the smallest of the baleen whales – which was still active four and half minutes after being hit by a harpoon in its rear end, and was probably still alive eight minutes after being struck. In the case of larger whales, the time may be thirty minutes or even more. Consider your reaction if you watched someone go into a field and harpoon a cow in the rump, which then took that long to die. In the light of present knowledge of these intelligent mammals, no civilized person can contemplate the whaling industry without revulsion and shame at the insensitivity of our own species.'

I encouraged people at the meeting to send telegrams to the Japanese and Russian Embassies. I believe the recent first-hand experiences, which I described, did something for my credibility with that great assembly. I also called for two minutes' silence, which was totally observed. At the end of it the voices of Humpback Whales came in to break the silence. When we got to the meeting we could not quite muster the voting power among the delegations to carry the moratorium proposal, and the exploiters were still allowed to kill too many Sperm Whales, and too many Bowheads could be taken, in the name of ancient tradition, by the native Alaskan peoples.

In the autumn of 1979 – three days after my 70th birthday – I arrived in Peking as leader of a team of five people from the World Wildlife Fund. Our delegation had been invited by the Government of the People's Republic of China to discuss international conservation matters, and the WWF was the first international body in that field to be so invited.

We were two weeks in China, the first in formal discussions in Peking and the second in north-east China, which used to be called Manchuria. There we were taken to the Chaingbai Shan – the Mountains of Everlasting Snow – where there is an excellent research station and a reserve of half a million acres of forest, believed still to have a handful of North-east Tigers (formerly Manchurian Tigers which are probably the same as Siberian Tigers).

It was getting late in the autumn and no doubt many of the summer migrant birds had already flown south. But we found very few birds, and only listed 38 species, although they included what seems likely to have been my first sighting of the Scaly-sided Merganser (*Mergus squamatus*), one of only two species of waterfowl which at that time I had never seen alive (the other is the Brazilian Merganser).

Back in Peking there were further agreements to be finalized, and a wonderful morning at the Zoo, when we filmed the Pandas and danced round a fountain with some adorable Chinese children.

We had brought with us a WWF flag about eight feet square and this we hung on the wall of the dry moat which keeps the adult Pandas in their enclosure. The flag is green, with a large version of my Panda symbol in the middle of it, and the cameras were ready to record any

Giant Panda. 1979. Oil on canvas. 12 × 10 in.

This little picture was commissioned by the World Wildlife Fund – whose symbol is a Giant Panda – for presentation to Premier Hua Guo-Feng of the People's Republic of China on the occasion of his state visit to the United Kingdom in 1979.

The picture was reproduced in a signed edition of 1,000 copies for sale in aid of conservation in China, and on each was reproduced the following message in the Premier's own calligraphy:

中国政府重视保护野生动物，並愿为此与世界各国合作。华国锋

The Chinese Government attaches great importance to the protection and conservation of wildlife and will co-operate with other countries of the world towards this end.

One of the results of my visit to China in the autumn of 1979 as leader of an invited team from the WWF was the initiation of a co-ordinated plan to help the apparently dwindling wild population of these delightful animals. There are perhaps between 400 and 1,000 Giant Pandas left in the high bamboo forests of Western Szechwan and Kansu Provinces. In 1977 there was a loss of 140 Pandas during the coldest part of the winter, possibly caused by a failure of the food supply, which is mainly fresh bamboo leaves. That is a serious loss, particularly if the total population estimate should prove to be over-optimistic.

During our visit to Peking in September 1979 it became clear that the Government was taking a new interest in environmental conservation, and that this included concern for the heritage of wild animals and plants still surviving in China.

Scaly-sided or Chinese Merganser. 1980. Black ink. Actual size of drawing.

Mandarins. 1957. Oil on canvas. 18 × 14 in.

Most people agree, when they look at a male Mandarin Duck in full plumage, that it **looks** Chinese (which of course it is). The plumage of **Aix galericulata** has probably not changed significantly in the last 50,000 years. If it is reminiscent of things Chinese, this is because Chinese culture has, during historical times, taken account of the Mandarin Duck and incorporated its amazing shapes and colours into all kinds of decorations. There is even a tradition of giving at weddings a pair of Mandarin Ducks in a cage as a symbol of marital fidelity. The drakes in the picture have raised their sails – each a single scapular feather – to a vertical position in display to the duck. No hybrid with the Mandarin Duck has ever been proved to exist, whereas the related North American Wood Duck or Carolina Duck frequently hybridizes with other ducks. The reasons for this appear to be that the chromosomes in the gonads are more numerous in the Mandarin than in any other ducks (84 in the male and 83 in the female against 80 and 79 in all others). Furthermore, all the Mandarin's chromosomes are straight whereas some are V-shaped in all other ducks. Japan's most distinguished ornithologist, Dr Yamashina, published his results on this subject in 1952 and proposed that, on chromosome grounds, the Mandarin Duck be placed by itself in a 'supergenus' **Dendronessa** – meaning tree duck, which reflects the bird's arboreal nesting and its tree-perching habits. But most authors still place it in the genus **Aix**.

reaction which the two-dimensional Panda might induce in the live animals. At one stage one of them sat down for a full minute and gazed at the image on the flag.

When we moved on to the enclosure of the young Panda, Yuan Zhin, which is the first successful product of artificial insemination in Pandas, it went up to the flag, playfully bit the edge of it, and then moved over and nuzzled the nose of the Panda in the flag. And all the time the movie camera was turning. The film is amazing, though no doubt it does not prove that Yuan Zhin considered the image to be another Panda. It seems to me, however, to indicate that there was some sort of recognition of the black and white pattern.

However, the significance of our mission to China had little to do with Scaly-sided Mergansers or the behaviour of Giant Pandas in the Zoo. It was a signal that China has recognized the importance of conservation in the context of development. We agreed formally to exchange people, information and materials; we agreed to develop and carry out co-operative projects in China, and to plan Chinese participation in international conservation activities; and we agreed to have a continuing link between the WWF and a newly formed body to be called the Society of Environmental Sciences of China.

A month later the Chinese Premier, Hua Guo-Feng, came to London on a State Visit. It was arranged that I should paint a picture of a Panda to be presented to him and that subsequently it should be reproduced as a signed limited edition with a statement about China's interest in conservation written by Premier Hua himself and reproduced below the picture in the print.

During the Premier's visit I was fortunate to be invited to meet him twice – once introduced by Mrs Thatcher at the official Government Reception held in the Banqueting House in Whitehall, and two days later at a luncheon at Buckingham Palace. On both occasions I was wearing a red WWF tie with Panda symbols on it and showed them to the Premier. On the second occasion, without any collusion, Prince Philip was wearing the same tie, and once more Mr Hua examined the symbol carefully. He duly wrote the message the next day, and it is reproduced in his own calligraphy under the Panda print.

Shovelers coming in to land. Date unknown. Black ink. Actual size of drawing.

Epilogue

Three ducks in a windy dawn. 1960. Oil on board. $9\frac{1}{2} \times 7\frac{1}{2}$ in.

In 1960 I needed at short notice a dust jacket design for my autobiographical book *The Eye of the Wind*, which was to be published the following year. It was a small painting on a board with a roughly primed surface. Both the priming and the paintings were done with vertical brush-work, which gives a certain cohesive texture to the little picture.

In a world so full of imponderables, how far ahead is it sensible to be thinking? One thing is certain: conservation is only meaningful in the long term.

I once rather sententiously dreamed up a 100-years rule. It said that for work you should seriously consider whether your activity was likely to make life better for someone in 100 years' time. Any time spent doing anything else was play or spare time stuff, of no real significance. Of course, it is an impossible rule to monitor. For example, how can you know what effect your children or grandchildren will have on their world, so time spent bringing them up may well conform with the 100-years rule. And the more one thinks about it, the more impractical it becomes. But sometimes, when choices come along I allow the question to flit across my mind. I find myself thinking about the Wildfowl Trust and what it can do in the long term at its various centres to bring a little sanity and peace into our lives.

The Trust's objects, in no particular order of priority, are conservation, research, education and recreation, and in all of these fields I am convinced it has something worthwhile to offer to the half-million people who visit its centres each year.

The Trust will, I hope, still be operating in 100 years. It has just acquired its first computer. Will that make it more, or less likely to be prospering in 2080? They tell me that computers can never be cleverer than the people who programme them. But what is clever? Never forgetting anything is a useful capacity. There is a scenario which starts with the fact that a computer can always win a game of draughts and will soon be sure of always winning at chess. It may not be long before we are using computers to programme each other and do virtually all our complicated thinking for us. So far they require people to mend them, and make new ones, but computers can easily be made to do both these things. At this stage there will be a symbiotic relationship between them and the human species; but they will have put so many people out of work that a Neo-Luddite Movement will be born, and people will go round with hammers destroying all the computers. But, of course, a few very small and very modern com-

Stormy weather – Pintails. 1957. Oil on canvas. 14 × 18 in.

A fresh wind out of the south-east as the depression goes by, and the Pintails come in with a rush. As the leading birds drop through the wind gradient their airspeed falls off and they have to flap, to avoid stalling. In his **British Birds** Thomas Bewick gave as alternative names the Pintail Duck, Sea Pheasant, Cracker or Winter Duck.

puters will 'crawl out of the woodwork' and start reproducing themselves. They will then get together and say among themselves, 'you know, these humans simply aren't reliable; we should probably liquidate them.' But then a magnanimous computer, whose ancestor had originally been programmed by a good and wise human, would chip in and say, 'don't you think the least we could do is to keep a few as pets?'

I should like to think that any descendant of the Slimbridge computer would hold kindly feelings towards the conservation of the human race. This leads me to ask the question whether, when a flying saucer finally lands on the earth and disgorges lots of little green men, they will be based on carbon, or silicon, molecules. And how does all this relate to SETI – the search for extra-terrestrial intelligence?

Speculation into the future is one thing; but I am also intrigued to speculate about – and investigate – present-day possibilities, like *Nessiteras rhombopteryx*, the name which Bob Rines and I gave to the Loch Ness Monster so that the animals could be adequately protected, if and when their existence was established beyond doubt. I am often asked, 'do you still believe in Nessie?' and my answer is, 'I keep an open mind, like all good biologists – all good scientists, come to that.' The lectures I gave on this subject were easily the most popular on the *Lindblad Explorer*. Our eldest daughter Nicola gave Phil and me T-shirts with the legend 'I believe in Nessie', and we used to wear them when we gave the lecture. This led our distinguished fellow lecturer Eric Shipton to wear for his lecture a T-shirt which said 'I believe in the Yeti', and to save production effort, his Phyllis wore one saying 'So do I'. But the great T. H. Huxley said, 'science commits suicide when it adopts a creed'.

Salmon at risk in Loch Ness. 1975. Oil on board. 15 × 18 in.

There is a curious consistency in the reports of the animals which so many people claim to have seen down the years in the loch. When all the deliberate hoaxes and the honest errors, the mis-identifications and the mass hallucination have been eliminated there remains a hard core of observations, photographs, films and sonar traces which seem to me inexplicable in terms of known phenomena or described animals. To provide legal protection for any undescribed animal in the loch, a scientific name must be published and this was done in the journal **Nature** by Robert Rines and myself in 1975. The name we devised for the species was **Nessiteras rhombopteryx**, the 'Ness monster with diamond-shaped fin'. Although I have spent many hours watching the loch and have dived three times in it, I have never had the good fortune to see a 'Nessie' myself, but taking all the descriptions and photographs into account, the picture gives my impression of what the animals may look like, if they are there. I still incline to the view that they are, but my scientific training demands that I keep an open mind. Without draining the loch (which will never be done because it is 27 miles long, more than a mile wide and 900 feet deep in places), it cannot be proved that no Nessie exists.

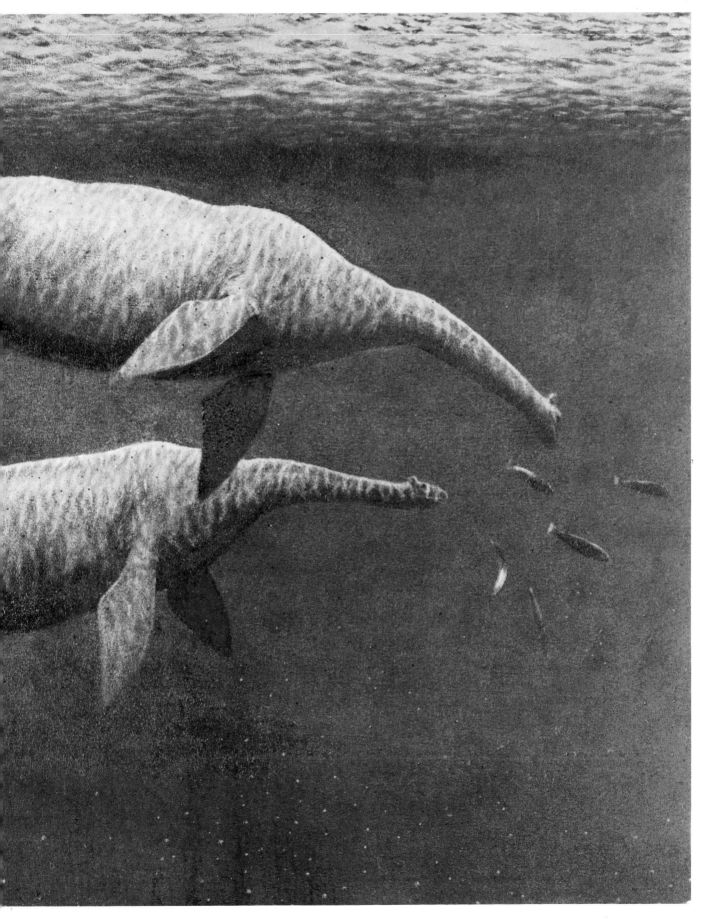

The patchwork quilt of this book must be brought to an end, and it should come back to the Wildfowl Trust at Slimbridge – to the new tower that we have added to our house, at the top of which I have been writing. There have been frequent interruptions from almost 300 wild swans, 1,800 wild geese and nearly 2,000 wild ducks who have been spending most of their time during December 1979 within a quarter-mile of the tower. This morning – the first morning of 1980 – it is frosty, and there is ice on the outlying water of Swan Lake and its 'back ponds'. The birds are concentrated within a hundred yards of me, all except the White-fronted Geese who have flighted two fields up from the Tack Piece, the fifty-acre grass field lying between Swan Lake and the Severn estuary, in which they and many of the Bewick's Swans spent all day yesterday and the day before, feeding in peace. Geese

Whitefronts at a freshwater roost. 1960. Oil on board. Size unknown.

This Scottish loch is a rather unusual setting for European White-fronted Geese, as this race is not common in Scotland; but the group, consisting of a family with three additional adults, quite possibly young of the previous year, has taken up residence for the time being in a place where one might much more probably expect to find their cousins, the Greenland Whitefronts.

Bewick's Swans over a pearly sea. 1975. Oil on canvas. 20 × 24 in.

These are the smallest of the three British swan species, the other two being the larger Whooper Swan which, like Bewick's, is migratory, breeding in more northerly countries, and the Mute Swan which is resident. The Bewick's Swans that come to the British Isles breed 2,000 miles away in the Soviet Arctic, arriving in October and leaving in March, or earlier in mild winters. The Wildfowl Trust has been making long-term studies of Bewick's Swans at several of its centres, based on the recognition of different individual swans.

may safely graze in these fields, and yesterday through the telescope in the tower I saw, among the 1,800 Whitefronts, two young Dark-bellied Brent Geese, five Pink-footed Geese, one young Bean Goose and a single adult Lesser Whitefront. With the swans scattered among them they looked superb in the low winter sunshine, and caused some loss of concentration on the completion of this book.

Ethology, the science of animal behaviour, has taught us that our own thought processes lie at the end of a continuum of rationality and exploratory initiative that stretches far down the evolutionary tree. One may watch young geese and swans playing with toys, nibbling at shoe-laces, 'dashing and diving' in mock escape from imaginary birds of prey; one may watch Red-crested Pochards, who make a speciality of playing with feathers, or Giant Pandas in a zoo, or wild Sea Lions

Peter Scott
1952

A Quiet place for teal. 1952. Oil on canvas. 30 × 25 in.

Teal that are resting undisturbed epitomize a peaceful scene. These nineteen are European Green-winged Teal in a quiet corner at Slimbridge. A sudden sound or movement and they would instantly take wing, constituting a 'spring of Teal'. It is arguable that they are always 'a spring' when they are in a small group – whether in flight, on the ground or in the water.

playing with ropes, or dolphins in an oceanarium, or one's own dogs, or one's own children. Who can doubt that these are points on a slope leading up to our species and hopefully to greater wisdom in the far future?

As I conclude this book in my tower on the morning of 2 January 1980, the day on which the manuscript must be delivered to the publishers in Oxford, I hear the news that a new pair of swans has arrived overnight. They are old friends, Lancelot and Elaine; in fact Lancelot is our oldest wild swan friend of all. He has been here every winter since 1963; this is his 17th consecutive year. Seventeen years is a long time (though Mrs Noah, our tame Bewick's Swan, is still alive at 32). Our Dalmatian is only fourteen and he is getting near the end of the road. It is one of the sadder things in human life that a dog's life-span should be so short.

'It is difficult to forecast,' runs the saying, 'especially about the future'; or, to put it another way, 'if you are not planning for the future, you should not be planning at all.' I have many plans – to paint, to listen to music, to illustrate another fish identification book, to continue to watch birds, and to show them and other creatures to people, to help with conservation, and especially to stop the slaughter of the whales.

Death, they say, is nature's way of telling you to slow down. I have no other plans for slowing down.

Self portrait of an artist writing a book at the top of a tower.
The Director's House at Slimbridge.

Peter Scott. 1980

Black ink. Actual size of drawing.

Red-breasted Geese and two Whitefronts. 1977. Ink and watercolour
in diary. Page 8 × 6 in.

I made this drawing in my diary after a winter's day in
Romania, when we had been hidden up-wind of the geese as
they landed less than 50 yards in front of us. It was the
nearest edge of a huge flock which was dispersed over a
1,000-acre field not far from Sinoie, south of the Danube
delta. In recent years we have become concerned about the
size of the world population of these beautiful little geese,
all of which breed in the Soviet Arctic, most of them on the
Taimyr Peninsula. It is possible that there are 20,000 of
them, though some fear that there may be no more than
half that number. For an intensely gregarious bird even the
optimistic estimate is perilously low. The time may come
when it could be worth considering the feasibility of estab-
lishing a free-flying feral population of them – perhaps in
the British Isles or Scandinavia, as a safety measure against
the danger of extinction.

Index

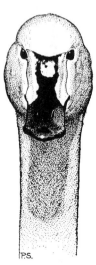

LANCELOT

1980. Black ink. About two-thirds of size of drawing.